The Intrapreneurship Formula

The Intrapreneurship Formula

How to Drive Corporate Entrepreneurship
Through Employee Empowerment

Sandra Lam

BUSINESS EXPERT PRESS

Leader in applied, concise business books

The Intrapreneurship Formula:
How to Drive Corporate Entrepreneurship Through Employee Empowerment

Copyright © Business Expert Press, LLC, 2023.

Cover design by Joyce Ng

Interior design by Exeter Premedia Services Private Ltd., Chennai, India

First published in 2022 by
Business Expert Press, LLC
222 East 46th Street, New York, NY 10017
www.businessexpertpress.com

ISBN-13: 978-1-63742-401-8 (paperback)
ISBN-13: 978-1-63742-402-5 (e-book)

Business Expert Press Human Resource Management and Organizational Behavior Collection

First edition: 2022

10 9 8 7 6 5 4 3 2 1

Corporate leaders who are facing disruption in their industry or businesses should read this book to understand how they can lead their organizations into the future era.

Description

Half of the industry-leading companies have lost their leading position in the last decade. Disruption across industries has been accelerated by the Industry 5.0 and the pandemic. One in every two companies might not be able to sustain its competitive advantage or even survive in the next 10 years. Corporations must innovate to keep themselves in the game. Yet, many corporations struggle at innovating. Only one out of five corporate leaders feel equipped to face the challenge. Corporate leaders have been told that their employees are valuable innovation assets. The key to building sustainable innovation is to empower employees and convert them into intrapreneurs. This book is designed to help the remaining 80 percent of the corporate leaders who struggle to lead innovation and intrapreneurship in their organizations.

This book offers a practical formula for doing just that—a guide to help leaders outperform and stay ahead of the competition in a rapidly changing environment. *The Intrapreneurship Formula* is created to help leaders plan and manage intrapreneurship in a structured way. The book introduces a tested formula that identifies and analyzes five key components of intrapreneurship that shape innovation activities in organizations across industries: Culture, Infrastructure, Traits, Skills, and the Network of Diversity. It can be applied to any organization or team to understand their strengths, as well as areas in which the current innovation ecosystem can be improved. The book helps leaders self-assess their current state and the areas of improvement and form a tailored plan to cultivate intrapreneurship. It is a simple but powerful tool for understanding the forces in the corporate ecosystem that are enabling or jeopardizing innovation. Corporate leaders who are facing disruption in their industry or businesses should read this book to understand how they can lead their organizations into the future era.

Keywords

intrapreneurship; intrapreneur; corporate entrepreneurship; innovation and entrepreneurship; innovation; innovator; corporate startup; corporate innovation; innovation management; innovation ecosystem; innovative leadership; design thinking; lean startup; agile

Contents

List of Figures

Testimonials

"If The Start-Up Way *by Eric Ries was your guide towards entrepreneurship in the era of Industry 4.0, Sandra Lam's* The Intrapreneurship Formula *is the perfect playbook to enable progress in the age of Industry 5.0. With actionable insights and inspiring case stories from her innovation career, I found this useful in decoding and guiding companies who are on a pivot-or-perish journey towards Intrapreneurship, Innovation, and Inclusion."*—**Soumee De, Partner, Workforce Advisory, EY**

"This book combines years of experiences Sandra has in the domain, key theories from other thought leaders together, to make a simple and easy to understand guide on how businesses, both large and small, can embark on the journey of intrapreneurship. The assessments and framework templates that are made available in the book make it really easy for anyone to apply in their day-to-day intrapreneurship activities. I highly recommend this book to any businesses, and teams who are new to entrepreneurship, and do not have much idea on how to start to pick up this book."—**Luke Goh, Director, Innovation Consulting, Salesforce**

"The world is changing, people want more from their jobs, and they want a sense of ownership in what they are building. This book gives a practical framework of how you can help your people grow the company from within. It's a win-win!"—**Monique D'Arcy, Senior Researcher, Microsoft**

"Today, most of us in this business world understand that innovation is one of the essential ingredients which endow a business organization with sustainable success. I believe many of us also have a meaningful experience with different sizes of business organizations in which we can find their people, various functions, and infrastructure that make us feel a culture full of innovation and creativity. However, we may not know exactly how these organizations

could build up such a lively phenomenon in their corporate environment. If you are seeking the secrets to this question, then this book is the right answer." —**Edwin Wong, Ex-Treasury and Credit Controller, Nike Greater China**

"In a time of rapid corporate innovation, Sandra's much needed The Intrapreneurship Formula *provides a practical approach to developing the right mindset. Her ideas and lessons are invaluable for any organization that is serious about differentiating itself to remain relevant in the future."* —**Sweatha Donkada, Distinguished Engineer, UBS**

"Using simple terms and ready-to-use toolkits, Sandra provides a practical, methodological guide on how to nurture innovation in an organization. A must-read for all business leaders who are determined to transform their companies."—**Alex Lau, Chief of Staff, Dah Sing Bank**

"As rapid innovation tops the agenda of corporates, this book provides pragmatic frameworks, case studies, and fundamentals for business leaders at all levels to leap across traditional approaches and implement innovation in their organizations."—**Shan Sharma, Corporate Innovation Consultant**

"Sandra Lam has written an insightful guide for business leaders aspiring to transform their organizations into innovative ones in the Age of Industry 5.0. It is full of important information, a pragmatic manual, and careful thoughts about change, innovation, and stakeholder empowerment."—**Yanbo Wang, Associate Professor of Strategy, HKU Business School**

"A must-have, must-read book for everyone, on every desk, offering experienced insights and step-by-step guided frameworks to pivot every business to a grounded innovation journey."—**Edgar Low, Ex-adjunct Faculty and Senior Practicum Manager, Singapore Management University, and Associate Lecturer, Ngee Ann Polytechnic**

Acknowledgments

I am extremely grateful to everyone who has helped me along my journey to get me where I am today. I am very thankful to people who have shared their ideas, thinking, and questions with me. Your generous sharing inspired me and enabled my learnings and growth. I appreciate all the great people whom I have worked with to put their trust in me to help them. In return, I have gained new knowledge and experience. I am very lucky to have known great leaders, key thinkers, and thought leaders in my field. All of you are amazing!

I want to thank my beta readers. I appreciate all the feedback you have given to me which shaped this book. Your input has helped me improve the book, making it more relevant to the readers.

I also want to take the chance to thank my spouse, Anthony, for his support and patience. For months I have been spending my after-work hours and weekends to complete this book. I am very grateful for having a spouse who encourages me to dream big and believes that I can do anything.

Finally, I want to thank the team of Business Expert Publishing for all of their support. Your team is very professional and I am glad about the trusted relationship that we have built.

Introduction

What would you do if you were told that your company will lose its competitive advantage or even go out of business in five years? What would you do today to save it? You might think of expanding into new markets, increasing margins, improving efficiencies, and cutting costs. But the truth is none of these incremental improvements is sufficient to save your business from the disruption that's happening all around us.

The world we're in today is experiencing an acceleration of technological advancement. We have seen disruption enabled by advancements emerging both in vertical markets and across industry sectors. The time taken to create and scale something from scratch is short—weeks, if not days. While these advancements bring opportunities, they also lower entry barriers. Leaders who have established businesses to run find themselves facing fierce competition from small startups that did not even exist a few years ago.

Most leaders know that innovation is important for their future success and survival, but few are satisfied with their current level of innovation. There is a gap between knowing about the need to innovate and knowing how to innovate. Some leaders simply do not know where to start. Some are struggling to innovate beyond traditional R&D. And some, especially those in large corporates that have invested a lot of resources, are wondering why they still cannot achieve the expected results.

Many failed because they drew on their experience of doing what they do best. They tried to run innovation the same way they ran their existing businesses. Others invested in external innovation experts who brought short-term excitement to the company. But once the engagement was over, they found themselves moving back to the old ways of doing things.

The key to sustainable innovation is to empower your employees and convert them into intrapreneurs. This book gives you a practical formula for doing just that—a practical guide to help you outperform and stay ahead of your competition in a rapidly changing environment.

This book will provide a guideline on how to assess the current level of intrapreneurship in your organization and identify areas for improvement. It will help you identify potential intrapreneurs and build a culture and infrastructure to nurture them. It will run through the training you need to provide your employees and how to attract and retain intrapreneurial talent. In short, this book will show you how to build a successful intrapreneurship program.

I've been a corporate innovation practitioner leading corporate innovation, intrapreneurship, and technology partnerships in corporates. I've helped C-suites develop strategies for sustainable innovation, built intrapreneurship programs, coached intrapreneurs, and transformed employees into founders.

This book draws on my experience of managing intrapreneurship and learnings from some of the world's most innovative companies. I've observed those companies change the way they approach innovation in the last few years. Traditionally it was through R&D centers with small, centralized teams. But more corporate leaders have come to realize that, to succeed, innovation cannot belong only to laboratories that are physically separated from the rest of the business.

In contrast, the teams that I have led built large-scale innovation practices for companies and seen the impact on both employees and the business. I have seen companies successfully launch new products based on the ideas of intrapreneurs. They turned into commercialization opportunities and drove new revenue.

Opening up innovation to employees also ignites their passion for the organization. They feel that they are involved and that their participation matters. I have seen employee engagement increase significantly. Of course, this doesn't happen overnight. Some corporates have taken months or even years to figure out how to implement intrapreneurship. Now, with this book, you have the formula to accelerate this transformation.

This book isn't a theoretical presentation nor a methodology for building a single product or new value proposition. It's designed for leaders who aspire to transform their organization into an innovative one by empowering their employees. It is a pragmatic manual that will help you deploy a sustainable approach to innovation.

My final message is: don't delay! Your direct competitors and others new to the field are innovating relentlessly to get your business. This book will give you a head start with its proven formula. Each chapter outlines crucial elements and actions, culminating in an action plan for managing intrapreneurship and generating new business growth. All by leveraging your biggest existing asset—your employees.

CHAPTER 1

The Demand for Intrapreneurs in the Age of Industry 5.0

Two decades from now, your company may not exist. That may sound like a downbeat assessment but I'm afraid it's a statistical likelihood. Since the year 2000, 52 percent of companies listed on the Fortune 500 list have gone bankrupt, been acquired, or ceased to exist.

Just as startling is the fact that, in just 10 years, half of the companies currently on the Fortune 500 list will be replaced.[1] It's a similar story with other leading share indexes. Back in 1990, the average tenure of companies on the S&P 500 was 20 years, down from 33 years for those founded in 1965.[2] It's still falling. By 2026, it's predicted that the average tenure of a company will be just 14 years.

This phenomenon is global and industry agnostic, and your organization is not immune. The question is: what will differentiate your organization from those that fail? How will it maintain its competitiveness and continue to thrive? The key is sustainable innovation. Only with innovation can a company constantly maintain its competitive advantage and grow its business.

Innovation is overused as a buzzword and the term itself can be very broad. People have tried to define it, however. When the entrepreneur and consultant Jorge Barba asked 15 leading innovation experts, they said that innovation involved new ideas, implementing them in a business, solving problems, and creating value for customers. My definition is slightly more precise. For the purpose of this book, I define innovation as the process of building a new product, service, process, or business model to create customer value.

Innovation is the ability to see change as an opportunity, not a threat.

—Steve Jobs

As an innovation practitioner, I have helped corporate leaders create value for their businesses by driving innovation. I have seen many of those leaders spend a tremendous amount on external consultants to create an innovation strategy, source new ideas, or organize innovation activities.

There's certainly nothing wrong with hiring external help. But it cannot stop there. Innovation is not something that can simply be outsourced to external parties. What's more, many leaders overlook one of the key assets of innovation they already have in their organization: their own employees.

By empowering your employees, you can drive innovation from within. Imagine that every one of your employees is a thought engine for your business, relentlessly exploring new value every day they come to work. Innovation at your organization would no longer be ad hoc; it would be continuous.

Employees who innovate are known as "intrapreneurs." The origin of the word isn't clear but it seems the idea was first mentioned in 1978 in a paper called "Intra-Corporate Entrepreneurship" by Gifford Pinchot and Elizabeth Pinchot. They were the founders of Pinchot & Co, a pioneering consultancy firm focusing on training for corporate innovation. In their work, Gifford and Elizabeth referred to intrapreneurs as "dreamers who do. Those who take hands-on responsibility for creating innovation of any kind, within a business."

You're familiar with the term "entrepreneur," which defines someone who builds a new business and takes risks in the hope of making a return. An intrapreneur is an employee who takes on the challenge of building new solutions or business models. They act like entrepreneurs while working in an organization.

In this book, we will discuss the importance of driving innovation via intrapreneurship and guide you on creating an ecosystem to cultivate it. This book will help you identify the resources you already have in your organization and where the gaps are. You will discover which employees have the potential to help your company thrive and the mindset, skills, and capabilities they need to become intrapreneurs.

Based on my experience and the knowledge of corporate innovators across industries, this book constructed a formula for you to successfully build the right culture. You will need to invest in the right inputs to form an ecosystem that results in sustainable intrapreneurship. We will discuss what the various inputs are, what they do, how to build them, and how to measure the outcomes.

Corporate Versus Startup Innovation

Entrepreneurship is the process that turns those ideas into actual innovations, and when it occurs in large corporations we tend to refer to it as intrapreneurship or corporate innovation.[3]

—Dr. Tomas Chamorro-Premuzic

Innovation in corporates versus those in startups looks quite different. The major difference is due to the presence of an existing business. Because of that, the challenges that startup founders are facing are vastly different from those of intrapreneurs. That explains why the ways how startup founders solve things may not always work best for intrapreneurs in corporates.

In a startup, innovation is a spontaneous process that happens continuously through a few passionate people bouncing ideas off each other, prototyping, and developing until it works. It is a trial-and-error process. Founders of a business know that struggle. They are facing extreme challenges including lack of funding, resources, and network. Starting from scratch, startup founders might not find themselves struggling with existing legacy, corporate strategy, and red tape. They are freer to imagine the future. They are also relentless because until the business is launched and takes flight, there is no return.

It is not the same in a corporate. Innovation in a big, complex organization is hard, in a different way. Employees are not hired to take risks but to execute and manage. The majority do not have innovation as their job scope. Trial and error might not be rewarded because the company hired you to do what you know, and so you do it the way it's supposed to be done. There are often established policies and procedures to avoid errors. Anything outside of the framework is seen as a deviation

Comparison	Corporate Innovation	Startup Innovation
Founders	Intrapreneurs	Entrepreneurs
Funding source	Corporate funding	Venture capitalists
Exiting clientele available	Yes	No
Talents availability	Employees in the corporate	Need to hire
Stakeholders' alignment	Highly required	Less of a concern
Legacy system to take care of	Yes	No
Bureaucracy	High	Low

Figure 1.1 *Comparison of corporate innovation versus startup innovation*

that might put the corporate at risk. Innovation is often something new being explored that does not sit well with the existing framework. For that reason, supporting innovation requires a long-term commitment from all levels, the redesign of processes and mechanisms, and disciplined execution. Without the right culture, skills, and infrastructure, innovation won't just happen. Figure 1.1 shows a comparison between corporate innovation and startup innovation, ranging from the types of founders to the bureaucracy they face.

Of course, you could always spend millions of dollars to get consultants to innovate for you and integrate it in-house. However, it is costly and not sustainable. The truth is that you have one of the strongest assets already: your employees. They are the ones who know your customers, business, strengths, and weaknesses. They know where the problems are and sometimes the solutions too.

Corporate leaders need to develop a pipeline of intrapreneurs who will innovate with new ideas and businesses. This book will provide a guideline on how you can achieve it. But first, let's take a short detour to examine the complex and rapidly changing environment in which innovation will take place.

Moving From the Industry 4.0 to the Industry 5.0

At the start of the 21st century, corporates have been busy dealing with a digital revolution that's often called "Industry 4.0." First introduced by Klaus Schwab, executive chairman of the World Economic Forum in 2015, its foundations were outlined in his subsequent book, *The Fourth Industrial Revolution.*[4] Industry 4.0 refers to technology that combines hardware, software, and biology and emphasizes advances in communication and connectivity.[5] It emphasized the interconnectivity of the machines, which increases efficiency and transparency in the workplace. The interconnected machines enabled the capturing and analysis of data of the end-to-end process. With the help of data, it allows decision makers to make better and quicker decisions and increase overall productivity. Given the abundance of data and the machines' capability to receive signals and react, the human's role shifts from an operator of machines toward a strategic decision maker and flexible problem solver. During Industry 4.0, emerging technologies including artificial intelligence, robotics, the Internet of Things (IoT), blockchain, and virtual reality (VR), and crypto have gained popularity and have been more widely applied in the world.

Industry 4.0 has already caused a drastic change in the business environment. Blockbuster versus Netflix is often cited as an example of how technology and a new business model can disrupt an industry giant. Blockbuster was the champion of video rental companies throughout the 1990s and early 2000s. At its peak, it had more than 9,000 brick-and-mortar stores globally.[6] But Netflix's cofounder, Reed Hastings, identified a customer pain point. Customers did not like paying late fees, which was one of Blockbuster's biggest revenue streams.

Netflix was launched in 1997 but did not take off immediately and Blockbuster did not consider Netflix as competition. In 2000, Hastings proposed a partnership but Blockbuster declined. But technology and business models soon changed. In 2007, Netflix transitioned from DVD shipments to online streaming. This led to exponential growth in subscriber numbers while Blockbuster struggled, eventually filing for bankruptcy in 2010. The Blockbuster versus Netflix example is one of the biggest nightmares for any corporate leader.

Blockbuster management was not visionary enough to see the opportunities in partnering with Netflix. On the other hand, I wonder what would have happened if an employee of Blockbuster had come up with the idea of online streaming. Would Blockbuster's management have acted on this breakthrough idea by recognizing its potential and helping the intrapreneur experiment and develop it? It could have been a whole new business model that kept Blockbuster in the game. But Blockbuster probably wouldn't have done it because it lacked the intrapreneurship formula to make it happen. And yet, Blockbuster was a profitable business for more than 20 years before it went bankrupt.

The pace of technological advancement back then was slower. Corporates nowadays might not have the same luxury of time. The change to digital technology has accelerated in the last two years and corporates are facing a more rapidly changing market environment than ever.

In the second decade of the 21st century, we have already set one foot into the era of Industry 5.0. Entering Industry 5.0 does not mean Industry 4.0 becomes redundant. We have to understand that Industry 5.0 is complementary to Industry 4.0. Industry 5.0 is the age of personalization, based on the digitization achieved in Industry 4.0. Industry 5.0 is putting humans at the center of focus of all technological advancement. While Industry 4.0 asked how can we digitize everything and make it seamlessly efficient, Industry 5.0 asks how can these digitized assets help humans bring more personalized services, build customized solutions, and create innovative experiences.

Industry 5.0 has a few key aspirations:

- Design of human-centric solutions: Leverage technologies to solve problems with a human-centric approach, to create the best experience for humans. It looks for solutions that build synergy and harmony between humans and machines. Robots are now shifting to "Cobots," which mean robots that collaborate with humans.
- Hyper-personalization: Data, once trapped in silos or not captured to detail, can now be collected, unified, and transformed into actionable insights in real time. Personalization increases complexity during the production process. However, with the automated, agile, and flexible production achieved by Industry 5.0, the highly personalized product can be prototyped within a short turnaround time.
- Focus on sustainability: Industry 4.0 did not have a strong focus on environmental issues. Industry 5.0 seeks better

technological solutions to achieve environmental protection. It leverages automation and artificial intelligence algorithms to increase sustainability in production processes.

The foundation of digitalization gave birth to vast opportunities for innovative products and services that can be produced on a mass scale yet unique to customers. Industry 5.0 aims not only to improve efficiency and transparency, but also to create a better quality of life for humans. It enhances the human factor of business, in terms of both customer services and operational processes.

Industry 5.0 Accelerated

There's no doubt that the world has changed since 2020. The impact of the coronavirus pandemic was felt around the world. As of March 2022, there were more than 456 million confirmed cases of COVID-19 and more than 6 million lives lost.[7]

The pandemic changed how we work, learn, travel, and interact with others. During the lockdowns and circuit breakers, outdoor activities were restricted and those who had safety concerns also opted to stay home. A year after the first outbreak, 56.8 percent of the U.S. workforce was working remotely, at least part of the time.

To stay connected with the external world and manage their daily lives, many sought to leverage technology:

- *Remote work infrastructure*. People who work from home rely on digital and video conferencing tools to stay connected with colleagues, collaborate, and get their work done without physically meeting.
- *Online shopping*. Many had to rely on online e-commerce to purchase groceries and necessities for daily life during lockdowns.
- *Contactless takeaway*. During the period when no dine-in was allowed, people ordered takeaway by digital means for either self-pickup or delivery.
- *Remote learning*. Students attended virtual classes from home.

- *Virtual fitness*. With the closure of indoor gyms and sports facilities, people exercised from home. Home-gym apps and online fitness classes gained traction.
- *Cashless payment*. Without visiting physical venues, most payments were made digitally. People used more cashless means, including credit cards and e-wallets. Merchants are moving their sales online, creating more demand for digital methods of collecting payment. Even in physical stores, due to hygiene concerns, people preferred contactless payments (e.g., payWave and QR codes).
- *Online entertainment*. Some 33 percent of Americans ranked streaming as the most important digital service during the COVID-19 lockdown, according to a survey by ExpressVPN. Of U.S. Netflix subscribers, 40 percent signed up for additional streaming services since the start of pandemic lockdowns.

Technology adoption will only accelerate as consumer behaviors change. Populations around the world, not just the born-digital generation, are getting into online retail, online payment, online entertainment, and more.

Corporations Need Innovation for Growth

In the age of Industry 5.0 and a pandemic, innovation is more critical than ever. It's not surprising that innovative companies outperformed their peers by around 10 to 20 percent in shareholder returns, both before and during the COVID-19 downturn.

Many companies have realized that now is the time to take action. This is reflected in a recent survey of companies' ability to adapt to the uncertain environment created by COVID-19. In its May 2021 report, "The Race for Innovation," Boston Consulting Group (BCG) reported that 75 percent of companies had made innovation a top-three priority for 2021.[8]

The fallout from COVID-19 is set to fundamentally change the way organizations do business over the next five years. This was the view of more than 90 percent of executives in a recent McKinsey study of 200 organizations across industries. Almost as many executives asserted that the crisis would have a lasting impact on their customers' needs.[9]

However, many saw opportunities too. Figure 1.2 shows that among leaders of various industries, more than three-quarters agreed that the crisis would create significant new opportunities for growth, with varied results in different industries. Take, for example, the technology industry: 85 percent of the executives expect the COVID-19 crisis to be a big opportunity.

It's clear that innovation is one of the key success factors that enable organizations to sail through crisis. In past crises, companies that invested in innovation delivered superior growth and performance in the aftermath.

In its report, McKinsey reviewed the market capitalization of the World's 50 most innovative companies recognized by Fast Company, both during and after the 2009 financial crisis. Based on Figure 1.3, these companies not only outperformed their peers by 10 percent during the crisis, but also outperformed the market by 30 percent in postcrisis years.

Unfortunately, many corporations had to focus on business continuity during the pandemic instead of innovation. Executives must indeed weigh cutting costs, driving productivity, and implementing safety measures against supporting innovation-led growth. However, in the long run, given the change in consumer behaviors, technology advancement,

Share of executives who expect the COVID-19 crisis to be one of the biggest opportunities for growth in their industry, %

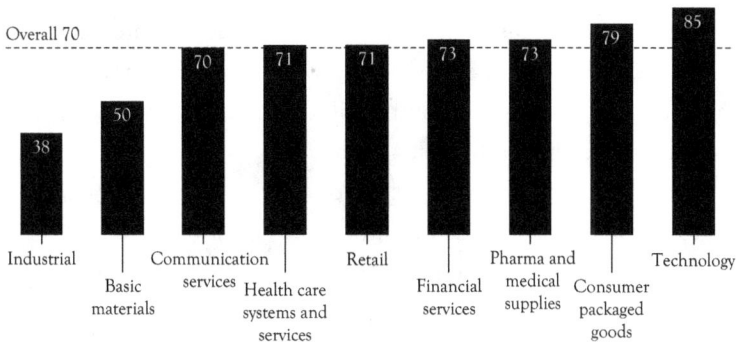

Figure 1.2 McKinsey Innovation Through Crisis Survey 2020

Source: McKinsey Innovation Through Crisis Survey, April 2020.

Normalized market capitalization, index (Q1 2007 = 100)

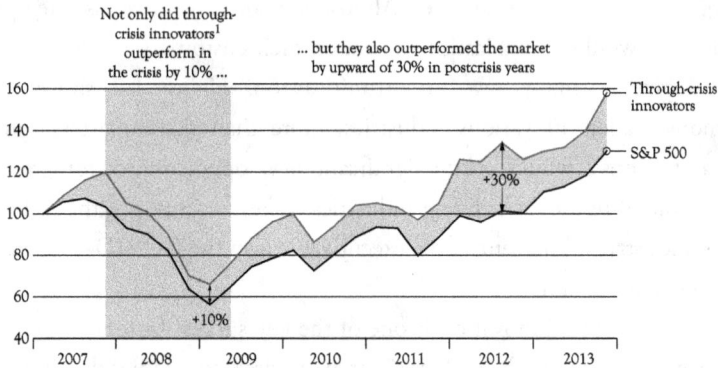

[1]Identified as companies on the Fast Company World's 50 Most Innovative Companies list for ≥2 years through a crisis, normalized to 2007.

Figure 1.3 McKinsey Innovation Through Crisis Survey 2020

and intensified competition, corporations will have to build a consistent innovation focus to create and maintain their competitive advantage. If you are the leader of a large organization facing disruption, your company's survival will depend on innovation. In turn, innovation will depend on your ability to harness the power of intrapreneurship. The time to act on this is now, before it is too late. Intrapreneurship is gaining in popularity due to accelerated changes in the market landscape. And yes, building this talent pipeline should keep you awake at night. Big tech giants like Facebook, Google, and Amazon have strong intrapreneurship cultures that make the majority of their employees intrapreneurs.

You might not see the immediate threat from this. Nor will you see an immediate return on investing in intrapreneurs. But compare a corporate that has only a handful of employees innovating to competitors that have the majority of employees innovating all the time. Which will still be in business and thriving in the next 10 years?

By now, I may have convinced you that you need intrapreneurs. So let's examine what they do in a little more detail.

What Intrapreneurs Do for the Corporate

Intrapreneur should not be an assigned, full-time job for an employee. And it is not someone hired only to innovate new ideas. An intrapreneur can be anyone. Intrapreneurs are given access to resources and assets in the established business and some autonomy to explore new ideas.

Within these parameters, here's how intrapreneurs should operate.

They Seek to Understand Future Megatrends

Intrapreneurs are interested in future trends in the market and businesses in general. They seek to understand trends on a large scale. They are good at taking in a lot of information and finding the relevant implications. They pick up signals showing where the industry is going and what competitors are doing. They expose themselves to external sources, including conferences, industry talks, and networking beyond the business, to proactively stay on top of the latest updates. They process information about the latest technology advancements to anticipate future changes in the business. They might see exciting trends that do not have an immediate impact on the corporate and sometimes are considered pure fantasy, as the trend is perceived to be so far away. Whereas most employees are saying "That's not going to take place for another 20 years," an intrapreneur will see it happening in five years.

They Analyze Problems In-Depth

Intrapreneurs look into the problems the corporate and the corporate's customers are facing today. They observe customers in detail to understand what they desire and hate. They do not see a problem as a given and would raise an eyebrow if they heard people say "That problem has been there since day one and it is how it is." They care about the problem they observe and have empathy with those experiencing it. They dissect the problem from various angles before jumping to solutions. They identify the pain point and try to understand the reason why it happens, where the friction comes from, and what it costs the users.

They Bring Big Ideas With Business Opportunities

Using the insights they have drawn from the problem, intrapreneurs brainstorm not only one or two but many alternative solutions. They would not limit themselves and would gather all possible solutions. Then they would evaluate which option is best. They are interested in big ideas that would solve the problem, delight customers, create value, and change the game. They are sufficiently savvy in business to apply a commercial angle to the solution.

They Execute and Deliver

Big ideas without execution are just thoughts. On the contrary, intrapreneurs are doers. Once they find a solution, they move on to an execution plan and relentlessly pursue it. They are extremely persistent and do not take no as an answer. They would form their team and gather resources by influencing others. They are good at removing roadblocks during the execution stage. They have a clear vision in their mind of what the outcomes would look like and what it takes to get there. They are strong performers who deliver results and will not stop until the results are realized.

Successful intrapreneurship can benefit the corporate in unexpected ways and make a tremendous impact on the business.

Intrapreneurship in Action: Ken Kutaragi and the Sony PlayStation

Ken Kutaragi is one of the most successful examples of intrapreneurship.[10] He joined Sony in 1975 and worked in the sound labs. One day, he bought his young daughter a Nintendo games console and noticed that she wasn't pleased with the sound quality. He analyzed the problem and concluded that the solution was to install a microchip dedicated solely to sound, which would significantly improve the gaming system. At that time, Sony was not in the gaming business. So Ken took the idea to Nintendo as an external consultant while still working for Sony. A life-changing moment came when Nintendo decided not to proceed with the project Ken was working on. But Ken understood both the market and the business opportunity and didn't stop trying to convince Sony to enter the gaming industry. Most of Sony's senior leaders didn't see the benefit. They considered Ken's computer gaming device a mere toy. But the chairman, Norio Ohga, recognized Ken's intrapreneurial spirit and took a big chance. The rest is history. Ken went on to lead the development of Sony's gaming system, which became the bestselling PlayStation.

Ken has demonstrated strong characteristics of an intrapreneur, that is, problem solver, obsessed with customers, always coming up with ideas, and so on. We will go into more detail about what makes a potential intrapreneur in Chapter 3. From there, you will learn more about how to identify the likes of Ken in your organization.

Another key takeaway from Sony's example is that Ken's success did not happen by chance. It was the result of both the disciplined innovation by Ken and the committed support of senior leader Norio Ohga.

Who Are Intrapreneurs?

Not everybody can be an intrapreneur. Intrapreneurs are people with a strong entrepreneurial mindset who are attracted to the idea of building a business. People with a strong entrepreneurial mindset do not often find themselves in a corporate. They like to explore freely, and they might not fit in with established workflows and systems. On the other hand, most employees do not join a company to create something new. Some 90 percent of employees simply do execution work.

It's also the case that intrapreneurs are not simply entrepreneurs who happen to work in a corporate.[11] Successful intrapreneurs need the drive to build a new business within the corporate and to navigate the complexities of the existing business. They have to be able to align with the corporate mission and strategy, navigate the politics when approaching senior leaders for sponsorship, and lead disciplined innovation practice (which is usually not the practice of the mainstream business).

An intrapreneur, then, is a refined version of both an entrepreneur and a corporate-savvy individual. Talents with intrapreneurial potential are scarce. They have some traits they are born with, and most can be learned. Later in this book, we will discuss how you can identify potential intrapreneurs and the skillsets they need for success.

Potential intrapreneurs come from all generations and backgrounds. Many would have believed that more senior employees are better intrapreneurs, given their expertise and experience. Knowledge and experience indeed play a major role in understanding the problem and finding the solution. However, your potential intrapreneurs can also come from less experienced talents, who are millennials and Gen Z employees in the workforce. Millennials have gone through the transition from the early stage of the Internet to an all-digital economy. They know what change is like and have seen it done. Gen Z was born digital and they expect everything in their life to be designed digitally. The following are further reasons why millennials and Gen Z employees are likely to be potential intrapreneurs:

They have been inspired by innovation brought about by technology companies. They saw how tech companies like Apple, Google, Facebook, and Amazon achieved great business success within a short timeframe. Many are inspired by the way these companies transformed our lives. The products and services these companies created and delivered have changed customer behaviors, including those of millennials and Gen Z. They are constantly comparing the standard of experience they get from these companies to any other product or service they get.

They are seeing the booming startup scene. Some of their peers are founding startups, joining startups, or shifting to join startups. These new companies provide an opportunity to leapfrog established companies and the potential to change the world. Those who join corporates want to experience the same "cool" things as their peers inside startups.

They are highly adapted to digital. Millennials have seen the digital transformation and Gen Z was born digital. They are exceptionally comfortable dealing with technology. Give them a well-designed digital product and they would be able to navigate it without an instruction manual. They are familiar with digital means of communication, entertainment, and work. They have instant access to limitless data and information via the Internet and social media.

Intrapreneurs are most often not at the top of the hierarchy; they could be spread across various levels and departments. Leaders need to find them, nurture them, and support their development to help the company innovate. But they are mostly overlooked by corporates, and this is a problem. If you can't create the right environment and structure for them to work in, you risk losing talent. Intrapreneurship was named the most desirable skill for 2020 by the global recruitment specialist Michael Page and high-growth companies are hungry for them.

Who Are Not Intrapreneurs?

We have discussed how technological advances are driving the trends of Industry 5.0. However, technology is only one type of innovation. It does not mean that intrapreneurs are technologists or researchers who only work in the research and development department.

Imagine that you are a skilled researcher and you know about the research work or the model that you are running inside out. You do your most productive work in the lab and you're driven to solve a particular problem. The moment people take you away from the laboratory and talk about using the technology for profit, you consider it beyond your scope. You cannot wait to go back to your actual work!

These persons may be fascinated to discover how science works, but it is obvious that they are not interested in building a new business out of it. It is not hard to see that this individual will not be motivated to become, or excel in being, an intrapreneur. There is nothing wrong with people following their hearts, doing what they are motivated to do. There is ample room for technologists to grow within their domain in a corporation.

Intrapreneurs might also not be the same people as high-potential leaders (Hi-pos). These are high performers who you identify as pipeline candidates for critical leadership roles like the C-Suite. Hi-pos and intrapreneurs indeed have many similarities in terms of mindset. They are high achievers and have a strong business sense. Hi-pos often have strong people-management skills and are put on the track to lead a large-scale corporate. On the other hand, an intrapreneur might not need to lead a large team. Innovation could, and usually does, happen faster in a team of a few driven people.

One key characteristic that distinguishes Hi-pos and intrapreneurs is their entrepreneurial spirit. While Hi-pos have to be comfortable managing an established large-scale corporate, intrapreneurs have to be comfortable dealing with the uncertainty and ambiguity of experimenting with new solutions.

Both Hi-pos and technologists can be potential intrapreneurs, given the right training and mindset shift. The point is that just because someone is tech-savvy, is a high-potential leader, or has deep-tech domain expertise, it does not mean they will make a great intrapreneur. Intrapreneurs can come from all domains and do not necessarily need a technology background. But they do need to be tech-savvy in the way they appreciate the technology, understand the concept, and see the potential business implications and risks.

How to Use This Book

Intrapreneurs are highly scarce, and they operate on different expectations compared to execution staff. They are full of ideas and seek satisfaction in creating change by realizing their ideas. You will lose intrapreneurs if your corporation does not allow them to create new things or businesses. That means your corporate will lose out, due to a lack of competitiveness. You will miss the business opportunities that intrapreneurs could have brought you. Alternatively, if you invest in intrapreneurs, they will pay your corporate back with a new product, solution, or business that justifies the investment. This book provides a framework and structure to help you identify and groom intrapreneurial talents to create new value. It will help your organization thrive and intrapreneurs to reach their full potential.

Sometimes, corporate leaders ask: "Will intrapreneurs ruin my business by taking too many risks?" No, they won't if you create the right ecosystem. This book will help you understand the components you need to build to help intrapreneurs grow without compromising productivity or risking your existing business. Innovation is an investment that requires commitment. Investment comes in the form of not only money but also effort from corporate leaders. If you don't have an ecosystem to support intrapreneurial talents, they will eventually leave to seek a viable environment in which they can thrive.

Make use of this book to create a pipeline of intrapreneurial talent and continue to upskill them. Work with your HR department to design an end-to-end employee journey for intrapreneurs. HR recruitment professionals need to know the importance of having intrapreneurs in the organization because they are the fuel that creates a future for the business. Corporate leaders and HR departments should join forces to transform the process of identifying, recruiting, and retaining intrapreneurs. Most of today's recruitment tools, including the aptitude test and interview methods, might not fully measure a candidate's level of intrapreneurship. Most do not even discover a candidate's entrepreneurial spirit, which is understandable. After all, if the person is so entrepreneurial, why would they come to interview for a job? But times have changed. Intrapreneurship is a new skill that is required for future corporates.

Throughout this book are assessment tools that you can use to evaluate your employees' current skillsets, understand their strengths and weaknesses, and build personalized training roadmaps for potential intrapreneurs. One key to success is to group intrapreneurs into cofounder teams. By building diverse groups of intrapreneurs in your organization, you can complement their skills and multiply the effect. Intrapreneurs can be employees from vastly different backgrounds and this book will help you understand the various types of intrapreneur profiles and exactly how they complement each other.

On the other hand, potential intrapreneurs also need reasons to join a corporate. A stable job with a rigid routine would not appeal to them. This book provides guideline to HR directors on how to find potential intrapreneurs, how to attract them to work for the corporation, how to train them with essential skills, and how to keep them motivated.

Finally, this book will discuss the pitfalls that can stop intrapreneurship and the boosters that can accelerate it. Take note of these practices and fill the gaps to ensure that your investment in innovation is not wasted.

In this chapter, we've seen how intrapreneurship is vital for driving innovation and innovation is crucial to the survival of corporations in the age of Industry 5.0. In the next chapter, this book will give you tools for assessing the level of intrapreneurship and the potential talent in your organization and practical advice on devising a customizable action plan.

CHAPTER 2

Let's Do a Pulse Check

You probably won't meet an executive who doesn't believe that innovation is vital for growth. In a survey by McKinsey & Company, 80 percent said it was very important or extremely important to their companies' strategies.[1] But only 6 percent were satisfied with their innovation performance and very few knew what the problem was or how to fix it.[2]

So it's not surprising that many leaders find it a challenge when it comes to describing and quantifying intrapreneurship. They ask, "Do I have enough intrapreneurs in my organization?," "Do they generate enough innovation initiatives?," and "Do I have a culture that nurtures good intrapreneurship?" These big questions are overwhelming and most often result in very vague answers.

In this chapter, we offer you with two assessment tests so that you can get started with measuring intrapreneurship in your organization. I have broken down complex and hard-to-measure innovation questions into simpler questions designed to assess the current state of your organization. These tests have been developed in partnership with innovation managers and corporate leaders.

For your convenience, you can download the assessments and templates in this book from my website: www.sandralam.me.

Figure 2.1 presents the first assessment, Level of intrapreneurship, in your corporate. This assessment helps you understand the level of intrapreneurship of your organization and identify potential areas of development to increase it further.

Figure 2.2 presents the second assessment, The intrapreneur in you. It is a self-test designed for individual employees. You can give it to employees who aspire to be intrapreneurs. Completing the questionnaire will help them better understand their strengths and give them insights on how to further develop their potential.

Assessment I
Level of Intrapreneurship in your corporate
(for corporate leaders)

This assessment will help corporate leaders evaluate the level of Intrapreneurship in their corporates. The results will also show the existing assets the corporate has and the areas of enhancement if they want to further develop Intraprencurship in their organization.

Review the following descriptions and consider how they apply to your corporate. Is this how others would describe your corporate? If you are a leader of a department or team, try the assessment based on the setting that suits you. Organization results could be different from standalone department or team.

Remarks: Please note that if you are providing ratings from a corporate leader perspective, this is your in impression toward the corporate. It might be an accurate assessment, depending on how well you know your corporate. To make it even more accurate, I would encourage you to have your employees provide the ratings. That would give you a truer picture of what your people think about the Organization.

Evaluate each statement and rate using the following scale:

1 = Not at all   3 = Often   5 = Always
2 = Only occasionally   4 = Most of the time

No.	Questions	Rating
1	We develop new product or solutions by anticipating the needs of customers even before they know about it.	
2	When we evaluate candidate for hiring, problem solving and creativity are some of the key areas that we focus on.	
3	Our employees are constantly contributing new product/solution/business ideas.	
4	We have a strong number of new product/solution/business launch year on year.	
5	Innovation is widely communicated and practiced in our organization.	
6	The no. of ideas generated by our employees are more than what we can handle and launch.	
7	We have a structured innovation process to validate new ideas by employees and progress them to launch.	
8	We proactively gather new ideas on products/solutions/businesses from our employees.	
9	We have clearly defined innovation metric, widely communicated, and reported in a timely manner.	

10	We are well aware of the challenges ahead posed by Industry 4.0.	
11	Our senior leaders believe in innovation and see innovation as a competitive advantage.	
12	Our employees feel that they can get to know people with different backgrounds easily in the organization.	
13	Our employees, upon coming up with the new ideas, know how to execute from scratch.	
14	Our employees are encouraged to raise new ideas and they are not afraid to do so.	
15	We engage our customers during product development phase.	
16	Our employees are respectful to each other. They appreciate new perspectives raised by others and view different opinions in a positive view.	
17	We provide trainings of future skillset that help our employees keep up with the technology trends.	
18	We have a sandbox environment for experimenting new ideas without affecting the business in production.	
19	We try our best to eliminate unconscious bias in hiring and performance evaluation process.	
20	New ideas are executed in a timely manner.	
21	We encourage our employees to collaborate cross-country, cross-department, and cross-functions.	
22	We provide avenues for people to pitch their ideas.	
23	We offer resources (including time) for employees to take up self-initiated projects which are aligned with the corporate goal.	
24	We are committed to building a diverse and inclusive workplace.	
25	Employees of different backgrounds are coming together to cofound and execute ideas.	
26	Our organization is ahead of the competition among all peers.	
27	We incentivize employees to innovate and reward innovation, be it success or failure.	
28	We offer trainings to upskills our employees to help them form, pitch, and execution big ideas.	
29	We create fair opportunity for everyone to have equal chance of success.	
30	Our employees are excited to contribute to the innovation of our organization.	
31	We have a well-established and widely communicated intrapreneur program, accessible to all employees.	
32	We have internal risk partners who act as enablers to innovation, instead of roadblocks	

(Continues)

(*Continued*)

33	Our senior and middle management are not "naysayers" (people who would say no to everything) to new ideas.
34	Our employees are empowered to provide value in new ways.
35	Our employees feel that they can bring their full-self to work and are highly engaged.

Level of Intrapreneurship Scoring

Look up the responses of the following questions in the aforementioned questionnaire. Write down your rating in the chart below. Sum them up to your total score. For example, in the sample score chart below, the total score is 12, which means the level of intrapreneurship in the corporate is "Low."

Your score

Question No.	Your rating
1	
4	
6	
10	
20	
26	
Total	

Sample score

Question No.	Your rating
1	1
4	3
6	1
10	4
20	1
26	2
Total	12

Score Interpretation

Your total score	Level of intrapreneurship in your corporate
26–30	Very high
21–25	High
16–20	Moderate
6–15	Low

Areas for development scoring

The following scores will provide you with insights on where to focus your time and energy to build an ecosystem of intrapreneurship. Transfer your ratings for each question based on the following charts and sum up the totals.

#1 Talents		#2 Culture		#3 Infrastructure		#4 Diversity	
Qn. No.	Rating	Qn. No.	Rating	Qn. No.	Rating	Qn. No.	Rating
2		5		7		12	
3		8		9		16	
13		11		18		19	
17		14		22		21	
27		15		23		24	
28		33		31		25	
30		34		32		29	
#1 Total		#2 Total		#3 Total		#4 Total	

Chapter 3	**Chapter 5**	**Chapter 6**	**Chapter 8**
The Potential Intrapreneurs in Your Corporation	Culture for Nurturing Intrapreneurs	Corporate Infrastructure for Cultivating Intrapreneurship	Network of Diversity

Chapter 7
Essential Skills of
Intrapreneurs

Chapter 9
Recruit and
Retain Intrapreneurs

Sample   I have built my personal brand

#1 Talents		#2 Culture		#3 Infrastructure		#4 Diversity	
Qn. No.	Rating	Qn. No.	Rating	Qn. No.	Rating	Qn. No.	Rating
2	4	5	4	7	3	12	2
3	2	8	2	9	2	16	3
13	1	11	4	18	1	19	3
17	3	14	2	22	2	21	3
27	1	15	2	23	2	24	5
28	2	33	2	31	1	25	2
30	2	34	2	32	1	29	3
#1 Total	15	#2 Total	18	#3 Total	12	#4 Total	21

Score Interpretation

In the example above, the corporate is strong at #4 Diversity and fairly good at #2 Culture. Its weakness is at #3 Infrastructure, followed by #1 Talents. Based on that, the corporate leader should prioritize turning these two weaknesses into areas of developments. To improve the corporate infrastructure, the corporate leader can focus more on Chapter 6 to explore what are the tools or practices have to be put in place to create an innovative environment. The corporate leader can also make use of Chapters 3, 6, and 9 to discover talent management for intrapreneurs.

Figure 2.1 Assessment I: Level of intrapreneurship in your corporate

How to Use This Assessment

- Work on the previous assessment and understand the level of intrapreneurship in your organization. Identify the current strengths and areas for development.
- Go to Chapter 3 to understand the traits of potential intrapreneurs. Make an inventory of the likely candidates in your organization. Reach out to them and discover their aspirations.
- Use "Assessment II: The intrapreneur in you" in this chapter, to assess your existing employees or potential candidates to discover their strengths and areas of development.
- Refer to Chapter 4 to understand the Intrapreneurship Formula for building an ecosystem for intrapreneurs to thrive.
- Read Chapter 5 to understand how to build the culture for intrapreneurship.
- Chapter 6 helps you set up the infrastructure for innovation, an environment that you need to provide for innovation to take flight.
- Chapter 7 lays out the key skills required for a successful intrapreneur. Evaluate your inventory (from Chapter 3) against those skills. See where the gaps are and make a learning roadmap to help them develop.
- Chapter 8 explains how the network of diversity brings more and better innovation.
- Use Chapter 9 to design an end-to-end employee journey for your intrapreneurs.
- Read Chapter 10 to avoid the pitfalls of innovation.

Next, you'll find Assessment II: The intrapreneur in you, which you can send to potential intrapreneurs. For employees who show a particular interest in intrapreneurship, give them a copy of this book so that they can learn more about the skills required.

Assessment II
The Intrapreneur in you
(for individual)

For individuals who are aspired to become an intrapreneur, this assessment will help them evaluate where they stand, what are their strengths and areas of development.

Are you a potential intrapreneur?
Review the following descriptions and consider how they apply to you. Is this how others would describe you? Rate yourself on each statement using the following scale:

1 = Not at all   3 = Often   5 = Always
2 = Only occasionally   4 = Most of the time

No.	Questions	Rating
1	I have many big ideas of new product/ solution/ business that can help my organization create new value.	
2	I can turn big ideas into reality.	
3	I take in vast information and can form my view around it quickly.	
4	I know the strategic focus of my organization and what innovation aligns with it.	
5	I am great at business pitching.	
6	I keep up with the mega trends and the latest technology that impact my organization, and the work that our competitors are doing.	
7	I know how to discover pain points of customers and come up with innovative solutions to address them.	
8	I know how to motivate people to work with me without direct authority over them.	
9	I am excited to meet various people from different background and learn about what they do.	
10	I am a good storyteller.	
11	I am obsessed with customers, and I seek to solve problem for them.	
12	I know how to validate ideas before I launch them.	
13	I have diverse social network and enjoy connecting with people of different backgrounds.	
14	I can identify people's strength and find ways to build on them.	
15	I am driven to learn and enjoy the process of learning.	
16	When I come up with a new idea, I can quickly identify relevant stakeholders in the organization who can help support the idea with resources.	
17	I adjust my communications style with different people.	

(Continues)

(*Continued*)

18	I like to challenge the status quo and find better ways of doing things.	
19	I am comfortable with navigating politics in my organization.	
20	I am comfortable with failure as it is part of the process of innovation.	
21	I am known for delivering exceptional results.	
22	I sometimes think about building my own business.	
23	I am comfortable with experimenting with new ideas.	
24	I am familiar with managing new product/solution/business development project.	
25	When things do not progress as expected, I identify the roadblock and address it quickly.	
26	I like to bring change and impact the world.	
27	I create win–win solutions for stakeholders.	
28	I am a good listener and am open to others' opinions.	
29	I can articulate my ideas and thinking process well.	
30	I rather act to learn than overanalyze.	

The intrapreneur in you scoring

Look up the responses of the following questions in the above questionnaire. Write down your rating in the chart below. Sum them up to your total score. For example, in the sample score chart below, the total score is 46, which means the likelihood that the person is a potential intrapreneur is "very high."

Your score

Question No.	Your rating
1	
7	
13	
15	
17	
20	
25	
26	
29	
35	
Total	

Sample score

Question No.	Your rating
1	4
7	5
13	5
15	4
17	5
20	4
25	5
26	5
29	5
35	4
Total	46

Score Interpretation

Your total score	Likelihood that you are a potential intrapreneur
40–50	Very high
36–45	High
26–35	Moderate
10–25	Low

Areas for developing scoring

The scores below will provide you with insights on where to focus your time and energy to reach your full potential as an intrapreneur. Transfer your ratings for each question based on the charts below and sum up the totals.

#A Disciplined innovation process		#B Leadership		#C Navigating the organization		#D Communications	
Qn. No.	Rating	Qn. No.	Rating	Qn. No.	Rating	Qn. No.	Rating
2		3		4		5	
8		9		10		11	
14		16		18		19	
23		24		22		32	
27		28		30		34	
#A Total		#B Total		#C Total		#D Total	

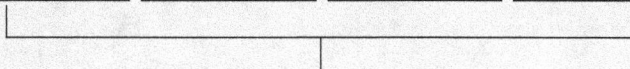

Chapter 7
Essential Skills of Intrapreneurs

Sample

#A Disciplined innovation process		#B Leadership		#C Navigating the organization		#D Communications	
Qn. No.	Rating	Qn. No.	Rating	Qn. No.	Rating	Qn. No.	Rating
2	3	3	4	4	4	5	4
8	2	9	3	10	5	11	3
14	2	16	4	18	4	19	3
23	2	24	5	22	4	32	3
27	3	28	4	30	4	34	4
#A Total	12	#B Total	20	#C Total	21	#D Total	17

Score Interpretation

In the example above, the person is strong at #C Navigating the organization and #B Leadership. The person's weakness are at #A Disciplined Innovation, followed by #D Communication. Based on that, this person should prioritize turning these two weaknesses into areas of developments. Refer to the skills under Chapter 7 "Essential Skills of Intrapreneurs."

Figure 2.2 Assessment II: The intrapreneur in you

Guide for Intrapreneurs Completing Assessment II

- Work on the assessment and identify your current strengths and areas for development.
- Read Chapter 3 to review the traits of potential intrapreneurs. Ask yourself honestly: Does it describe who I am? Do I aspire to be a person like this? Decide for yourself whether you want to be an intrapreneur. You can change your destiny.

Getting Started

- Review your "Areas of development" scores and refer to the relevant skills described in Chapter 7. Decide which skill is the most important or impactful for you to expand first.
- Design a personalized learning plan based on the priority skills you need to acquire.
- Start a short weekly review session (you only need 15 minutes) to evaluate your progress and improvement.

Build Momentum

- Learn, practice, evaluate, and repeat.
- Practicing what you have learned is essential for you to reach your goals.
- This book will help you learn about the skills required for intrapreneurship. To master them, you should explore resources that can help you dive deeper and sharpen those skills. Refer to the external resources recommended for mastering each skill.

This chapter has provided you with a great starting point in the form of two assessment tools. The scores from Assessment I show you the level of intrapreneurship in your organization. They will guide you on the existing strengths and areas for improvement. You can then proceed to tackle specific areas by reading the relevant chapters of this book. Each chapter has detailed guidance on practices to build, enabling you to form a customized action plan for your organization.

Based on Assessment II, you will have engaged some of your employees to assess their potential to become intrapreneurs. In the next chapter, we'll discuss the traits of potential intrapreneurs in more detail. You will see how the assessment is designed to discover these traits. It will make it easier for you to identify the talents with whom you interact in the future, without requiring them to do a detailed assessment.

CHAPTER 3

The Potential Intrapreneurs in Your Corporation

Creativity is just connecting things. When you ask creative people how they did something, they feel a little guilty because they didn't really do it, they just saw something. It seemed obvious to them after a while.

—Steve Jobs

You might not know it, but you have more potential intrapreneurs in your company than you think. To help you identify them, in this chapter we'll discuss the common traits potential intrapreneurs will have. However, that does not necessarily mean that this group of people has all the skills required to be successful intrapreneurs.

Use the exercise in this chapter, "Make an intrapreneur inventory," to start making a list of potential talent. In Chapter 7, "Talents: Essential Skills of Intrapreneurs," you will learn how to evaluate their skills systematically and how you can help them maximize their potential. Your job is to provide the training, the culture, and the infrastructure to help them grow.

Employees who aspire to become intrapreneurs should have these traits. Traits are not skills but natural abilities. They are who you are. Traits explain what we do and why we do it. Potential intrapreneurs should ask themselves: Is this who I am, or do I enjoy being someone like this? Those born with these traits will be naturals when it comes to acquiring the skills to become successful intrapreneurs. Those not born with these traits can develop them if they are willing. They can be acquired through a mindset shift.

Everyone is at a different stage in their intrapreneurship journey. The most important thing is to understand where an employee is now and how they can develop themselves.

Traits of Potential Intrapreneurs

Intrapreneurs have eight key traits:

1. *Problem solver*

   Intrapreneurs are natural problem solvers. They are comfortable in embracing the fact that there is a problem and acknowledging it. They will identify the problem, break it down, and analyze the root cause. They will then move on to exploring the solutions. They are good at finding the broken parts in a product, process, or system, and do not mind getting their hands dirty to find ways of doing things better.

2. *Always curious*

   I have no special talent. I am only passionately curious.

   —Albert Einstein

   Intrapreneurs have a high curiosity quotient (CQ). CQ refers to having a hungry mind.[1] Intrapreneurs are curious about anything and everything. They have a natural desire to discover and explore. They are attracted to new things, new people, new activities, and new experiences. They always ask questions from various perspectives to dig deeper into the issue. They seek to understand how things work. People with higher CQ are also more tolerant of ambiguity, which is often seen in the innovation process.

3. *Full of big ideas*

   Sometimes they are seen as dreamers. They talk about big trends, exciting opportunities, and crazy and radical ideas that others might not find easy to follow. They look for inspiration in various and unexpected places. They learn from other industries or fields and find connections between things and experiences. They are intrinsically motivated, instead of being forced to come up with new ways of doing things. Not all their ideas will be great but they keep exploring nonetheless.

4. *Bias toward action*

Intrapreneurs do not stop at just having an idea. They have a strong bias toward action that pushes them to act quickly and move the idea forward. When no one can decide on a new idea, they will act to test it out and come back with learnings. They are comfortable acting with "good enough" information and focus more on taking the action to progress than being perfect.

5. *Natural collaborator*

Intrapreneurs might not be deeply knowledgeable in a specific domain but they know how to connect the dots. This also works in terms of putting people together or connecting with them to understand the various perspectives of a problem or finding out the solution. They respect the inputs of people from different backgrounds and seek to stitch the pieces together.

6. *Constantly learning with a growth mindset*[2]

Because intrapreneurs are highly curious, they are self-driven to learn new things and skills. They are people with a growth mindset. They believe that they have control over their ability and can improve via learning. They see learning as a fun activity and enjoy the process of learning. They are also comfortable with not knowing and seeing opportunities from it. They are motivated to explore how things work and are proactive in seeking new knowledge.

7. *Challenge the status quo*

This group of people does not say "It is just how things have always been done." They would not simply accept that the existing method is the best and the only method. Ask them to do the same thing twice more and they will get bored and try to find an alternative, often even better, way of doing it.

8. *Lead without permission*

Because intrapreneurs have a high level of curiosity in diagnosing problems and finding relevant solutions, they will not ask for permission to take the lead. They would reach out to connect with people, assemble resources, and influence others to build the solution. They do not see themselves as individuals with a single reporting line, only working within their scope.

If employees believe they have these traits, they have the potential to be an intrapreneur. If not, they should ask themselves: Do I aspire to become someone who possesses these traits? If so, that person is also a potential intrapreneur.

The good news is that traits can be taught and acquired with practice and discipline. There will be human inertia, of course. That person might have been in a specific thinking mode their whole life. But with determination and action, they can change.

Some people are born more intrapreneurial than others. Those with a more intrapreneurial spirit are naturally better at, or more comfortable with, the role but it is also a self-fulfilling prophecy. The better they are at doing it, the more relevant skills they acquire to make it happen. In return, that brings positive results, which boost their confidence as an intrapreneur even more. For people who are not born intrapreneurial, here is the good news—intrapreneurship as a skill can be learned and sharpened through practice.

The fact is that even a born potential intrapreneur needs to devote a lot of hard work to make themselves a successful one. Everyone has a different starting point. What they need to focus on is how to get better.

One of the traits of intrapreneurs is having a growth mindset. That means they believe they can be trained and learn continuously. In the section "Exercise: Find the Potential Intrapreneurs," you'll find an exercise you can give to potential intrapreneurs in your organization that will reveal their existing skills. You can follow the links to subsequent chapters that discuss the skills in greater detail.

Leaders aren't born, they are made. And they are made just like anything else, through hard work.

—Vince Lombardi, American professional gridiron football coach

Intrapreneurship in Action: Ford's On-The-Go H2O

Intrapreneurs like Doug Martin build big ideas by connecting the dots. Martin was a powertrain controls engineer at Ford. He had read about a billboard in Lima, Peru, that condenses water in the air into drinking water in a dry environment. The billboard produced 2,500 gallons of water in three months, dispensing it to the local community who did not have access to clean water. He was fascinated by the idea of applying the same idea to cars since air runs through automobiles too.

A couple of years later, in 2015, Ford ramped up its global innovation challenges.[3] In the challenges, it seeks new ideas from beyond the research department, across the whole company. A total of 4,500 employees submitted their innovation ideas. Among them was Doug Martin's idea On-The-Go H2O, which condenses air from vehicle air conditioners to produce drinkable water.[4] Doug partnered with a colleague, John Rollinger, to prototype the idea. They found that a single vehicle can produce more than 64 ounces of water each hour, equivalent to four bottles of water. Not only did the project provide drinkable water from cars to combat water scarcity, but it also encouraged consumers to purchase less bottled water. On-The-Go H2O was selected and supported by Ford's management. It was brought to life in an advertising campaign, "Try On-The-Go H2O," and was a finalist in both the Transportation and Developing World Technologies categories in Fast Company's 2017 World-Changing Ideas Awards.[5]

Make an Intrapreneur Inventory

Now that you know the traits of a potential intrapreneur, you need to identify employees who possess these traits in your organization.

When it comes to identifying intrapreneurs, their corporate rank does not matter. They need not be a managing director or have any senior title to make them a successful intrapreneur. Intrapreneurs operate on a flat hierarchy as they are resourceful and persuasive enough to make others follow their lead. In fact, most of the time you can find potential intrapreneurs in middle-ranking or even entry-level positions. They must have some experience in the industry or organization or else you might find them challenging everything without any in-depth insight. At the same time, they might not have too much experience which makes them inflexible at thinking outside the box.

You should start with the teams with which you interact to identify these talents. If you want to identify a wide pool of talent, it's best to involve your human resources department so that they can provide you with a list.

To find talented individuals in your company who might become intrapreneurs, leaders and managers should ask:

1. Who always comes up with new ideas?
2. Who is constantly learning new skills and sharing with others?
3. Who tries to bring together different departments and functions to solve a problem?
4. Who is passionate about driving change in the organization?
5. Who always puts in the effort to bring their ideas to life?

Who are the people that spring to mind? Write down their names. This is the list of assets you have in your organization. They might not possess all the essential skills at the moment to become successful intrapreneurs. But what they have is the right attitude to be an intrapreneur. To help them succeed and create value for your corporate, you will have to provide them with training, support, and the right environment.

Exercise: Find the Potential Intrapreneurs

Write down the list of names that come to your mind using the list of traits and the questions earlier to build your inventory. Depending on the level of intrapreneurship in your organization already, you might or might not have a full list to start with. That's okay. Making your inventory is just the starting point.

My potential Intrapreneurs

1.	6.
2.	7.
3.	8.
4.	9.
5.	10.

11.	16.
12.	17.
13.	18.
14.	19.
15.	20.

If you're struggling to write down any names above, you might be wondering whether there are any potential intrapreneurs or innovative employees in your organization. If that's the case, it could be that there is a lack of talent in your organization. But the situation might also uncover deeper issues in your organization that you are not aware of.

When leaders claim that their employees are not creative enough, it is seldom the employees' fault. Innovation needs to be supported by an ecosystem. When there are no fish in the pond, you will have to find the root cause. Is there no water in the pond? Is the water level too low? Is there enough food? And so on.

If you're lacking names on your list, I recommend that you refer to the "Areas for development scoring" under Assessment I: Level of intrapreneurship in your corporate in Chapter 2 to understand the reasons.

You should also work with your managers and HR department to understand the situation at the organizational level. Here are a few questions that will help you start to understand the causes:

1. Does the corporate culture support innovation by employees?
2. Do we provide the right environment for ideas to be heard and experimented with?
3. Do we provide the right training and development for our employees to come up with and execute big ideas?
4. Are our employees inspired to innovate by diverse networks in the organization?
5. Do we know how to keep intrapreneurs motivated to retain them?

All of the above matter. Discover the areas of development that your organization should pursue to increase the level of intrapreneurship and you will be able to attract, retain, and even discover talent in your organization that you never expected.

Intrapreneurship in Action: McDonald's Happy Meal

Combining a hamburger, small fries, a drink, and a kid's toy, the McDonald's Happy Meal has been one of the company's greatest revenue generators. It was launched in 1979 following an idea by an employee in Guatemala, Yolanda Fernandez de Cofiño.[6] McDonald's was one of the favorite places for parents to bring their kids after school and other activities, and Yolanda observed their interactions. When parents were mingling and catching up socially, their kids were bored. To keep the kids entertained, Yolanda came up with an idea, the "Menu Ronald," which combined a hamburger, small fries, and a small sundae as a package.

The idea came to the attention of Dick Brams, a St. Louis marketing manager. He contacted Bob Bernstein, who ran the marketing agency for McDonald's.[7] Bob further developed the idea into the "Happy Meal," refining the components of the meal and marketing it nationally. It was launched to huge success. The Happy Meal has evolved, given changes in customer tastes and preferences, but the concept remains the same. According to estimates by Sense360, an insights firm with a panel of over 2 million anonymous consumers, 14.6 percent of customers who visited McDonald's ordered Happy Meals, and the company sold roughly $10 million worth of Happy Meals a day in August 2016.[8]

The Happy Meal has been on the menu for more than 40 years and is still going strong. It all started with an employee thinking about putting a few components of a meal together.

In this chapter, we discussed how you can identify the potential intrapreneurs in your organization. If you have completed the exercise, you will now have a list of names to target. These people are among the first that you can groom to become intrapreneurs as they have the natural traits to start with. It does not mean that other employees of yours can never become intrapreneurs. Intrapreneurship can be trained, as we will discuss further in Chapter 7. However, there are more factors at play than just having natural talents. To enable innovative behaviors, you need to build an ecosystem that nurtures intrapreneurship. In the next chapter, we will discuss the components such an ecosystem requires and how to build one.

CHAPTER 4

Introducing the Intrapreneurship Formula

In the last chapter, we have discussed how to identify intrapreneurs in your organization. The bad news is that, despite drawing up a list of potential talent, you can still fail miserably at corporate intrapreneurship. Many people think that some corporates are more innovative than others because they have more innovative leaders or employees. That might be true, but it's not the whole story. Having a group of talented intrapreneurs is only the first step in building toward successful intrapreneurship.

In this chapter, we will discuss what it takes to induce an organizational change, that is, the ingredients of the formula of intrapreneurship. This formula is created to help leaders plan and manage their intrapreneurship strategy in a more structured way since many do not have a well-formed one. The Intrapreneurship Formula is a formula that identifies and analyzes five key components of intrapreneurship that shape innovation activities in organizations across industries and helps determine the organization's level of innovativeness. The Intrapreneurship Formula can be applied to any organization or team to understand their strengths, as well as areas in which the current innovation ecosystem can be improved. It helps leaders form a tailored plan to cultivate intrapreneurship to enhance the organization's long-term competitiveness.

The Intrapreneurship Formula is a business innovation analysis model that helps to explain why various organizations sustain different levels of innovativeness. It is a simple but powerful tool for understanding the forces in your ecosystem that are enabling or jeopardizing innovation. Based on that, you will be able to adjust your intrapreneurship strategy accordingly.

A corporation is a type of organization composed of a collection of people in pursuit of defined objectives under the same corporate environment. Psychologist Kurt Lewin, one of the pioneers of social, organizational, and applied psychology, claimed that human behavior is a function of the person and the environment the person is in.[1] It can be expressed in the form of an equation. The desired behavior in this instance is intrapreneurship.

$$Behavior = Person \times Environment$$

It is a simple equation that provides a good starting point to discover what drives intrapreneurship in an organization. According to Kurt Lewin, "person" refers to the individual's characteristics.[2] It is similar to the concept of traits discussed in Chapter 2.

"Environment" refers to various aspects of an individual's situation at the time of the behavior, including their physical surroundings and social environment. Therefore, the actual behavior of a person depends on the person's characteristics and the temporary structure of the existing situation. There is no distinction between which of them, heredity or environment, is more important.

Lewin's theory also said that heredity and environment must work together to effect a certain mode of behavior. This is because the variations in behavior shown by people with the same individual characteristics may be extremely large. Having innovative people is important but it's only part of the equation. The environment, where the innovative people are working, is equally important.

In this book, I'll refer to the interaction of individuals and the corporate environment that they are in as the "ecosystem." So what are the components of a viable ecosystem that facilitates and sustains the behaviors of intrapreneurship? Let's extend the concept of Lewin's law and apply it to intrapreneurship. In this instance, the desired behavior is the intrapreneurs' desired behavior of innovation.

Environment

Let us start with the component environment in Lewin's theory. In this instance, we are referring to the environment where the desired innovation behaviors are conducted. In their book, *Innovation As Usual*, Paddy Miller and Thomas Wedell-Wedellsborg point out that the primary job of the leader is not to innovate.[3] Instead, it is to become an innovation architect, creating a work environment that helps people engage in the key innovation behaviors as part of their daily work.

The job of an architect is to design the space and the surroundings with which people will interact. An experienced architect would observe the existing environment (including sunlight, wind direction, and landscape), understand the functions and expected human activities, and integrate them to design the building, rooms, corridors, and even the doorways. Good architecture should follow the principles of firmitas, utility, and beauty. It should be robust and sustainable, useful, and function well for the people using it. It should delight people and raise their spirits.[4]

Imagine that this architect is you, the corporate leader. To design an ecosystem for corporate intrapreneurship, you will have to:

1. Observe the existing corporate environment.
2. Understand the function of innovation and the expected innovative behaviors.
3. Come up with the design, from the concept to the details.

And what does good architecture tell you about an innovative ecosystem?

- It should be sustainable.
- It should work for the people who are innovating within it.
- It should create emotional delight for people to engage.

To further analyze the environment that nurtures innovation behavior, I have broken it down into two parts: culture and infrastructure.

Environment = Culture + Infrastructure

"Culture" refers to the amalgamation of values, vision, mission, and the day-to-day aspects of communication, interaction, and operational goals that create the organizational atmosphere.[5] Culture affects every aspect of the corporation, including how decisions are made, who gets hired, and how people interact both internally and externally. In Chapter 5, we will discuss what creates a culture that nurtures intrapreneurship and what shuts it down. We will talk about:

- What is the culture of fear and how does it affect your innovation activities?
- What might your people be afraid of?
- How do you check whether there is a culture of fear in your organization?
- How do you create the culture for intrapreneurship?
  - How does customer obsession help innovation and how can you increase the customer focus of your employees?
  - How do you communicate innovation with your employees?
  - Why does failure management matter and how do you handle failures?

The second element under environment is "Infrastructure." Infrastructure comprises the basic systems and services an organization uses to work effectively. In the context of this book, infrastructure refers to the combination of business design and process that enables intrapreneurship to happen. Innovation in large corporates needs to be managed with a disciplined process that requires systematic management. Chapter 6 will provide a breakdown of the key components of the organizational infrastructure and answer questions including:

- How do you manage your employees' ideas?
  - How do you capture ideas?
  - How do you align the ideas with your strategy?
  - Who should evaluate the ideas?
  - How should you handle new ideas that might cannibalize your existing business?
- How do you manage innovation as a portfolio?
- What IT infrastructure do you need to enable the execution of new ideas?
  - How does cloud computing help speed up innovation?
  - Why do you need a sandbox?
  - Why do you need to empower your employees using data?

- How do you measure intrapreneurship? What are the key metrics?
- How do you safeguard the intellectual properties of the new ideas during different stages?

We will be discussing all the aforementioned in Chapter 6. Using the information, you can assess the current infrastructure of your organization and identify what assets you can leverage and what you need to build to enhance the level of innovativeness.

People

People are the true assets of your organization. For innovation behaviors to occur, people are a major component.

In Lewin's law, "people" refer to employees' characteristics. In the context of this book, I have defined the function of people in three key components: traits, skills, and network of diversity:

$$People = (Traits + Skills) \times Network \ of \ Diversity$$

"Traits" explain what drives a person's decisions and actions. In Chapter 2, we have discussed the traits of intrapreneurs. Using the information in Chapter 2, you can understand the characteristics, abilities, and thought patterns associated with successful intrapreneurs. That will help you identify the existing potential intrapreneurs in your organization.

But traits alone are not sufficient to drive innovative behavior. In the context of corporate innovation, there is another aspect of people besides their characteristics: "Skills." Skill is the essence of an employee doing something well. It is the ability of employees, based on their knowledge, practice, and experience.

You can view traits as the driving force behind a person wanting to become an intrapreneur, while skills are the determining factors of whether they can become a successful intrapreneur. Employees might be curious and dare to explore, but without the right skills, they won't be able to carry out innovation activities and successfully innovate. Either they would have to acquire the skills through experience or leaders would have to provide them with access to the means of developing them.

In Chapter 7, we will dive deep into the essential skills of intra-preneurs. Once you identify the right candidates, there is a list of skills that you need to help them acquire. These skills include disciplined innovation, leadership, navigating a large organization, and communications:

1. Disciplined innovation process:
   - How can the employees identify a problem with business value?
   - How can they validate the problem?
   - How can they approach and break down a complex problem? How can they build a solution concept?
   - How can they validate the solution concept?
   - How do they move ahead with limited resources?
   - How do they manage the pace of innovation work?
   - How do they move at speed and deliver innovation with a quick turnaround?

2. Leadership:
   - How can your employees lead by influence?
   - How can they lead through volatility, uncertainty, complexity, and ambiguity during the innovation process?
   - How can your employees network widely and across disciplines?

3. Navigating a large organization:
   - How do your employees manage a wide group of stakeholders with different motivations?
   - How can they get stakeholders' buy-in?
   - How can they deal with resistance to new ideas within the organization?

4. Communications:
   - How can your employees communicate complex innovative concepts to various stakeholders?
   - How can they sell a product that is not launched yet?
   - How can they effectively build a story around a new idea to convince people to invest in it?

With these skills, you can prepare your employees to become successful intrapreneurs who can go forward on their own to discover problems, develop solutions, and collaborate with and persuade other stakeholders to move forward.

Employees in a large organization never work alone. People achieve results most often through teamwork. Leveraging the partnership formed by an employee with other employees creates a network effect to achieve more and better ideas at a faster pace. Intrapreneurs are not limited to a single background or domain. In Chapter 1, we discussed how anyone can be an intrapreneur. With different backgrounds, knowledge, and practices, different types of intrapreneurs bring different values to an intrapreneur team. In Chapter 8, we will discuss the role the network of diversity plays in intrapreneurship, including:

- What are the different types of intrapreneurs by profession and character?
- What value do different types of intrapreneurs bring to the table?
- How can you help your employees form an all-rounded intrapreneur team?
- How can you help different types of intrapreneurs communicate better among themselves?
- What is the ideal size of an intrapreneur team?

By reading Chapters 2, 7, and 8, you will be able to identify the potential intrapreneur candidates, provide them with the right training, and help them form highly effective teams to create new business value for your organization.

Bringing It All Together: The Intrapreneurship Formula

Combining the above, sustainable intrapreneurship becomes a function of people's traits and skills, and the culture and infrastructure created by leaders as an environment.

> # The Intrapreneurship Formula
>
> Intrapreneurship = ((Traits + Skills) ×
> Network of Diversity) × (Culture + Infrastructure)

Figure 4.1 helps visualize the Intrapreneurship Formula and how the key components interact.

In this chapter, we've broken down the ecosystem of intrapreneurship into its components of traits, culture, infrastructure, and skills. So let's dive in and examine how to build each of these components. In the next chapter, we'll discuss the factors that determine a culture that nurtures innovation.

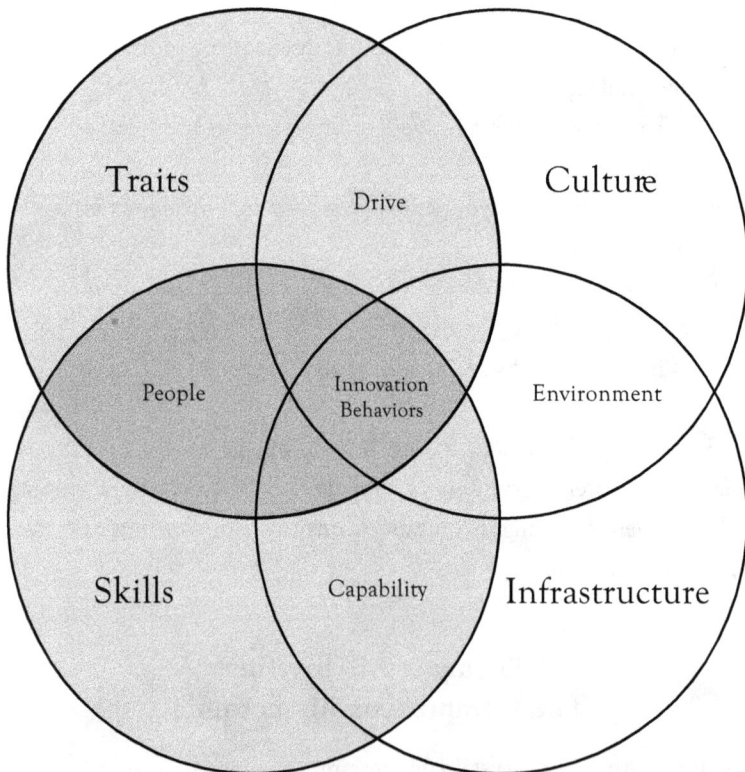

Figure 4.1 The Intrapreneurship Formula

CHAPTER 5

Culture for Nurturing Intrapreneurs

Have you ever led a meeting in which, after speaking for 45 minutes, you invited your team to suggest ideas? You waited. There was complete silence in the room. For a minute, no one said anything. People avoided eye contact with each other and tried their best not to make a sound. After slightly more than a minute, you could not bear it anymore and ended the meeting. People were relieved and left.

In her book *The Fearless Organization*, Amy C. Edmondson discusses employees who fail to speak up due to fear.[1] She referred to that as the dangerous silence. Dangerous silence is often observed in large organizations when employees are not willing to tell truths, offer suggestions, or give an opinion.

It could be caused by different reasons: Your employees think you are the one who decides everything, they don't care, they don't think that their voice matters, they don't think that you can make ideas happen, and so on. Listen to the dangerous silence—it is a call to leaders saying it's time to fix the culture.

I worked as an innovation coach in a large corporation. When I landed my job, one of my tasks was to make innovation mainstream. I was hired to encourage employees to innovate more routinely, instead of just focusing on business as usual. To understand the current state of the corporation, I participated in various meetings to observe the dynamic. I have seen dangerous silence quite often in multiple settings.

Eager to understand why and how it developed, I approached a diligent member of staff, Fred (not his real name). Fred was a dedicated, engaged employee whose performance was outstanding and who was excellent when it came to customer relationships. He delivered a great performance in project work but was always silent during meetings. I had built trust with him over some work engagements so I reached out to him and had a one-to-one chat. I asked him for his thoughts on the topic the team discussed in the earlier meeting.

Fred felt that the current plan for the new product would not work, based on his interaction with customers. I asked what he observed from the customer interaction. He slowly opened up and shared his ideas on how to resolve the problem. I was excited to hear them and, from the conversation, Fred sounded like a potential intrapreneur who had great ideas to contribute and create value for the company.

But still, I wondered why he didn't say a word during the meeting. Fred did not take a second and replied with a laugh, "Well, I have a 3-year-old kid." I was confused. How is not contributing idea associated with having a kid? I asked him to walk me through his thought process. Fred paused, searching for the link he made from one thing to another. He said,

> I have a 3-year-old kid; I cannot risk my job. I am not sure whether my boss welcomes my ideas. Maybe my idea was not that great—I don't want to embarrass myself. I am not sure if the idea would work. If it doesn't work out, it might backfire on me. So why should I bother?

I sat there digesting his words. I realized that this was a pattern that Fred goes through in his mind every time he has an idea. Fred became so familiar with this logic that it didn't even take him two seconds to run through it and tell himself to swallow that idea down his throat.

Why should you, as a corporate leader, care what Fred thinks? Because when you have one Fred in your organization, you lose the brilliant ideas of one person. But if you have 20,000 Freds, you have a culture of Freds, and that in fact is the culture of fear.

Culture of Fear: The Thief of Innovation

Everything you want is on the other side of fear.

—Jack Canfield

Many people have experienced culture of fear in their organizations, especially in large, complex corporations. Living in a culture of fear, people are uptight and afraid of making mistakes. All the focus is on execution according to the rules, without deviation, as failure is almost not acceptable. The culture of fear makes employees focus on survival by achieving their daily goals. New ideas, which come with uncertainty, are simply not appreciated.

Somehow Fred, in his statement, spelled out the reason that leads to the culture of fear. Let's break it down.

I am not sure whether my boss welcomes my ideas.

Fear of Disapproval

Employees are afraid to speak because they are concerned about the response they will get from their boss. It could be due to previous experience if employees have received cold or hostile feedback on ideas they have raised in the past. But it does not always take an actual experience to form this fear. When the management culture is strong on opinions, intimidating, or disapproving, it could also make people feel that any idea will not be welcomed and so they decide to keep their heads down.

Maybe my idea was not that great. I don't want to embarrass myself.

Fear of Not Being Good Enough

Some employees have low self-esteem and are not confident about their idea, no matter how good their idea is. They could be asking themselves, if this idea is so great, then how come no one thought about it? They think that they are not in a position to suggest good ideas as they are not experts in the field nor are they smart ones. They worry about how others will view them and their idea if their idea sounds stupid to others. Aside from the employee's characteristics, this could also be caused by some past incident of being dismissed or belittled by people working with them.

I am not sure whether my idea works.

Fear of Uncertainty

In the *Harvard Business Review* article "Why Employees Are Afraid to Speak," James R. Detert and Amy C. Edmondson interviewed around 200 employees from all levels and functions of a leading high-technology corporation.[2] The corporation had numerous formal feedback mechanisms, including an ombudsperson and a grievance procedure, to proactively encourage people to speak up about problems. Yet the interview results showed that half of the employees felt it was not safe to speak up or challenge traditional ways of doing things. The findings also revealed that the perceived risks of speaking up felt very personal and immediate to employees, whereas the possible future benefit to the organization from sharing their ideas was uncertain. To play it safe, people tended to keep their mouths shut.

It might backfire on me so why should I bother?

Fear of Punishment

This is about the motivation of innovation. As a corporate leader, you might think that your employees are asking, "Would I be rewarded for coming up with new ideas?" Well, your employee's question in fact might be "Am I going to be punished if my idea does not work?" Pitching new ideas takes courage and it can put you at risk. If you think about it from your employees' perspective, it all makes sense. I have dedicated my time and effort to doing something that is beyond my work scope and I don't even know whether it will succeed. Will my manager see it as a waste of my time? If it does not work out, how is it going to affect my performance review? The employees would only be willing to expose the idea if they feel confident and safe in the environment.

Does Your Corporation Have a Culture of Fear?

As a corporate leader, it might not be easy for you to spot a culture of fear, even if it is happening under your nose. Many leaders have mistakenly recognized the culture of fear as a strong alignment in the organization.

If you want to find out whether your corporation is operating under a culture of fear, ask yourself the below questions.

Are you Always Surrounded by "Yes Men"?

You might think that you have done an amazing job because people working for you always say yes to you. You think that you are smarter than them so they have to listen to you. They always agree to your ideas simply because your ideas are better. That might not be true. It could be that your people know that you do not like to be challenged. They might think that you have decided on your own way, so why should they bother? Or it could be that, over time, you have unintentionally chosen to be surrounded only by people who say yes to you. Malcolm Gladwell highlighted in his insightful book *Outliers: The Story of Success* that having people on teams or in organizations who are afraid to challenge each other can be extremely detrimental and even deadly.[3]

Are you Talking 75 Percent of the Time or More During Meetings?

Sometimes leaders are eager to share their vision and strategy with the team. They want the team to know what they are trying to achieve and how they think it should be achieved. Communication is good. But one-way communication is not. If you notice that you are the one who is doing most of the talking, you might be a terrible meeting lead. Over time, your employees might just assume that you will do all the talking and they will become disengaged. Notice the dynamics next time you walk into a meeting.

Do Your Employees Only Do Things by the Book?

When was the last time you saw an employee come up with a new way of doing things? Does that happen often in the company? Or are people only doing the same thing in the same way? When you talk to your team, notice how they mention rules and policies. It is good that they value rules in the workplace as they keep an operation organized. But overemphasizing it could become mechanical and paralyze thinking, as people are concerned about the consequences of breaking the rules. Your employees might follow the rules without understanding them. Review whether you have implemented a lot of unnecessary rules. Having too many of those can discourage people to think outside the box.

Questions for corporate leaders:

- Are you surrounded by "yes men"?
- Are you talking 75 percent of the time or more during meetings?
- Do your employees only do things by the book?

Create the Culture for Intrapreneurship

Amazon is probably the company that is most famous for its obsession with customers. Jeff Bezos ranks customer obsession as the number one leadership principle at Amazon.[4] The principle reads, "Leaders start with the customer and work backward. They work vigorously to earn and keep customer trust. Although leaders pay attention to competitors, they obsess over customers." Amazon even implemented meetings with an empty chair reserved for the customer so that employees always have customers in mind during the meeting.[5] Customers should be your corporation's most important stakeholders. Each employee, no matter whether they are front, middle, or back office (even those who do not have direct contact with customers), should always have the customer in mind when they carry out their job. Every decision should put the interests of the customer first. You can start creating customer obsession in your organization by doing the following.

Incorporate Customer Obsession Into Your Principles

Does your corporation have a set of principles in place? Review those principles. Is the customer part of the content? Do your principles emphasize that the customer is at the center of everything? Your leadership principles represent the core values of your corporation. They help the employees to understand what the corporation stands for and what takes priority when a decision is to be made. Include customers in your principles and widely communicate them with your employees. Here are some examples:[6]

- Google's company philosophy #1: Focus on the user and all else will follow.
- HubSpot culture code #2: We obsess over customers, not competitors.
- Uber cultural norms #2: We are customer-obsessed.[7]

Capture Data-Driven Customer Insights

Conventionally, companies use demographics to segment their customers by age, gender, income, occupation, location, and so on. Each segment is assigned with an overgeneralized set of characteristics and typical preferences. In the age of Industry 5.0, data are much more available and keep growing. With abundant data, you can get to know each of your customers in more depth. Data give you a full, transparent, and unbiased picture of your customer.

> It really doesn't matter if you are a 60-year-old woman or a 20-year-old man because a 20-year-old man can watch Say Yes To The Dress and a 60-year-old woman could watch Hellboy.
> —Todd Yellin, VP of Product Innovation at Netflix[8]

Data can be either quantitative or qualitative. Quantitative data are often easier to be discovered and analyzed. However, qualitative data are equally important for understanding customers. Unlike quantitative data, qualitative data might not offer you direct numerical value. Qualitative data are more narrative. They offer you patterns and insights into more complicated questions. Qualitative data provide you with a more comprehensive picture of your customers' behavior. They also offer you the opportunity to understand how your customers make their decisions and the reason for their behaviors. If you want to build data-driven client-centricity, try the following step-by-step approach:

1. Map out the customer journey with each touchpoint.
2. Every touchpoint with the customers presents a data opportunity. Understand what data are associated with the touchpoint.
3. Decide what data would be meaningful for you to understand the client better.
4. Capture the selected data points continuously and review them regularly for insights.
5. Adjust your strategy, products, and customer service based on the data insights.

Question for corporate leaders:

Review your corporate principles. Are your customers part of them?

Intrapreneurship in Action: Amazon Buy With 1-Click

In the era of online shopping, the conversion from browsing to buying is important.[9] The attention span of an online shopper is rather short. It's easy for shoppers to get distracted by other things. Sometimes a shopper finds a better product, sometimes they return and are no longer interested, and sometimes they just never come back again. So to achieve a higher conversion rate, the design of the checkout process needs to be as frictionless as possible. Amazon founder Jeff Bezos has always been obsessed with customers and he discussed the idea of a frictionless order system over lunch with Peri Hartman, an Amazon programmer who joined in 1997. Jeff believed that customers should be able to buy something just by clicking on one thing. The idea sounded simple and neat but it was not available on any of the e-commerce platforms. Hartman took this seed of an idea and ran with it. Eventually, he came up with a mechanism that enables the customer to check out with, literally, one click. To activate the one-click option, the system retrieves a customer's identification and payment methods from their first-time purchase and inputs it into the system the next time they look up a product. Hartman filed a 10-year patent for this checkout process in 1997, which gave Amazon a major advantage in the e-commerce industry against its competitors.[10]

Share and Celebrate Customer Stories

A story is a powerful communication tool that you can use to influence and inspire people. Strong stories help people connect. Discover the real stories of how your product or service changes a customer's life or day. Tell those authentic stories to your employees and celebrate success. Stories bring corporate purpose to life.[11] By sharing stories, employees feel that their work impacts real people. It also inspires other employees to take action that aligns with similar values.

Starbucks has been doing a phenomenal job sharing its customer stories. It has created a platform, Starbucks Stories And News, and made it available not only to employees but also to the public as a great marketing tool.[12] One of the stories that went viral really touched me. Krystal Payne joined the Starbucks store in Leesburg, Virginia, in 2016 and she noticed a frequent customer, Ibby Piracha, looking frustrated as he tried to place an order. Piracha is deaf.[13] Piracha generally places beverage orders by typing them into his phone and showing the barista. Krystal wanted to do something more to make him feel more welcomed. She came up with an idea—to learn and practice American Sign Language (ASL) outside of her work hours. She finally mastered the relevant signs and one day when Ibby walked into the store, she wrote him a note that said, "I've been learning ASL just so you can have the same experience as everyone else." Piracha offered a smile of appreciation for Payne, who proceeded to make the beverage he ordered. It might not be a life-changing experience for the customer but it certainly created a delightful moment. If you keep celebrating these extra miles that your employees go for customers, it helps other employees to understand the priorities of your corporation.

Question for corporate leaders:

Can you think of a delightful customer story in your corporation?

If you want your team to innovate, you need to create a culture of intellectual bravery, in which members are willing to disagree, dissent, or challenge the status quo even when they risk being embarrassed, marginalized, or punished. This doesn't happen overnight. Rather, employees must go through several stages along the way to that point.

In his book *The 4 Stages of Psychological Safety: Defining the Path to Inclusion and Innovation*, Timothy R. Clark broke down the stages required for people to feel psychologically safe. They have to feel (1) included, (2) safe to learn, (3) safe to contribute, and (4) safe to challenge the status quo.[14] Innovation happens when stage 4, challenging the status quo, is achieved. To get there, a leader has to help the team increase intellectual friction and decrease social friction.

Watch Your Body Language

Have you ever worked for a leader with a strong power of authority who allowed no one to challenge them? There was just such a senior managing director with whom I worked in my previous career. She had more than 30 years of experience in the industry and was highly respected. Her experience, knowledge, and network made her think that she was always right. At that time, I was a middle-level staff member at the company, reporting to a director, and this managing director was my manager's supervisor. She made it clear to her one-downs that, in her meetings, no one except her one-downs should speak. I was told by my manager that I was in no position to provide any comment or feedback. Even when her one-downs spoke, they were mostly interrupted or cut short by her and were told that their opinions were wrong. After a few encounters, no one even made the effort to express an opinion different from hers. A year later, most of the team members had left the company.

Some leaders might not realize that small gestures can create fear. Interrupting someone in the conversation, tapping your fingers on the table, rolling your eyes, looking at your watch, or ignoring someone during a meeting can send dismissive signals. These gestures can make people feel belittled. Sensing that they are not the ones in power, they retreat into silence and hold back from sharing their thoughts. Figure 5.1 shows examples of dismissive body language that leaders should avoid.

Question to corporate leaders:

Reflect on your interaction with your team during past meetings. Have you displayed any dismissive gestures? Did you feel your audience held back from talking?

Invite in a Way That People Can Respond

To help your employees to participate or contribute ideas, leaders need to invite and offer them the opportunity. Some leaders would say, "I have already asked over and over again whether anyone has an opinion. It's just that no one responded." I do not doubt that those leaders have asked the question, but how they asked also matters. First, the invitation needs to be genuine. To start with, when you invite participation, it has to be sincere. Acknowledge that you do not have all the answers in the world and be humble to learn from your employees. When your employees contribute their opinions, listen with patience. Recognize opinions positively and acknowledge the person's effort. Ask incisive questions to clarify the

Examples of dismissive body language	
• Tossing the document • Walking out • Heavy-lidded glances to a person • Heavy sighing • Eye rolling • Distracted self-grooming • Looking at your watch • Shrugging • Disgusted laughing • Using a mobile device instead of paying attention	• Palms together, looking upwards as a prayer position • Breaking eye contact or turning away to look at someone else • Dropping things on the table intentionally • Counting fingers • Engaging in sidebar conversation • Asynchronous head shaking • Talking while departing

Figure 5.1 Examples of dismissive body language[15]

idea, help build it further, or connect the dots with others with similar initiatives. Examples of the invitation could be:

- I am not an expert in this area. Does anyone here have experience or knowledge of it?
- We can all learn together by sharing information and past learnings.
- I appreciate your honest feedback. Do you have any suggestions of how we might address this?
- That is a good idea! How can we help develop it further?
- The idea is interesting. It helps address some of the problems we have. Can I clarify how it works?

It will not be an overnight process. People need to build trust with leaders to open up. The leader's job is to provide a safe space for them to respond and contribute.

Build Inclusion

For intellectual bravery to happen, people first need to feel that they are included. You might be asking, "How could they not feel included since we belong to the same corporation?" Being in the same company and feeling included are not the same thing. Feeling included is not just about having an access pass that allows you to walk through the door and more about the social signals you get from people around you. Can you recall an experience of feeling excluded? A teacher ignored your point of view, a boss called your idea silly, or your team went for drinks without inviting you. All these experiences make the person feel small and would also make them close up as they think they don't belong to the group.

When people feel that they are included, they know that they have a seat at the table and that their voice will be heard. According to a Salesforce report,[16] "The Impact of Equality and Values Driven Business," employees who feel their voice is heard at work are nearly five times (4.6×) more likely to feel empowered to perform their best work. Inclusivity has other benefits as well. In Bersin by Deloitte 2015 High-Impact Talent Management research, Josh Bersin surveyed and interviewed more than 450 global companies to identify their level of maturity in a wide variety of talent practices. It is found that more inclusive companies were 1.8 times more likely to be change-ready and 1.7 times more likely to be innovation leaders in their market.

As a leader, you might not be able to observe all exclusions that are happening in the workplace all the time. What you can do is to start to understand what inclusion means to your corporation, be the role model of inclusion, and start building inclusive. Here are a few things that you can do:

- Be aware that everyone has an unconscious bias.
- Notice who has not spoken during the meeting and invite them to contribute.
- Show respect to others' ideas.
- Admit that you might not always be right. Apologize if you make a mistake.
- Avoid jumping to your conclusion too fast.
- To further build inclusion organizationwide, consider inclusion training to educate your people managers.

Intrapreneurship in Action: Dreamworks— Inclusive Intrapreneurship

When it comes to innovation, some departments are always left behind compared to others as they might not be seen as the "creative" ones.[17] Examples include departments like finance, human resources, risk, compliance, legal, and so on. But not at Dreamworks. Dreamworks has been a leader in technological innovation that is at the forefront of shaping the entertainment industry. It has brought the world inspiration through its Shrek and Madagascar series. At Dreamworks, no one is left behind for innovation. It values creative input from every employee, even accountants and lawyers. It actively solicits ideas and receives creative thoughts from all workers. Dan Satterthwaite, head of Human Resources, has said that regardless of an employee's job role, they are provided training on how to pitch their ideas, whether it is a new movie or a better plan for developing new products. Dreamworks also provide avenues for anyone in the company to pitch their ideas to

(Continues)

(Continued)

a panel of the executive team, who listen to and assess them. Dreamworks has built an inclusive culture by opening the door of intrapreneurship. It lets employees pitch a movie concept, gives all workers access to artist-development courses, and allows them to take risks and learn from mistakes instead of firing them.

Communicate Openly and Consistently About Innovation

Communication is an important foundation for innovation. Your employees need to understand your corporate strategy and focus to make a meaningful contribution. Every meeting, every town hall, and every newsletter is a great opportunity for leaders to openly talk about innovation in the organization. Corporate leaders need to communicate regularly about:

1. Their long-term commitment to innovation.
2. Why innovation is important?
3. Why do they want the employees to be part of the innovation force?
4. What kind of innovation they would like to focus their energy on?
5. The assets that the corporation can provide to accelerate innovation.

The communication should be consistent for both internal and external audiences. If the message that employees get internally is different from what they see in the public, it creates a discrepancy. Employees could start to question the leaders' commitment and discount the internal message. Make sure your external marketing message is aligned with your message to staff.

Questions for corporate leaders:

- How often do you communicate innovation to your employees?
- Are your external and internal messages about innovation consistent?

Encourage Wide Collaboration

Silos usually occur in a large organization. Employees are given a set of tasks and they interact with the people those tasks require them to. And yet collaboration is a key element of sparking innovation. In Google's report "Working Better Together," the company surveyed senior staff and C-suite executives from over 250 companies representing a wide range of business sectors and sizes.[18] An overwhelming 73 percent of respondents agreed that their organization would be more successful if employees were able to work in more flexible and collaborative ways. Some 56 percent of respondents ranked a collaboration-related measure as the number one factor impacting their organization's profitability.

The number of collaborators is important too. Nielsen's report, "How Collaboration Drives Innovation Success," claimed a positive relationship between the number of people actively working on a new product idea and its performance with consumers.[19] Ideas developed by teams of three or more people have 156 percent greater appeal to consumers than those developed by teams where just one or two people played a hands-on role. The report also found that organizations that consistently achieve high levels of collaboration on product concepts can substantially improve their competitive advantage and revenue.

Wide collaboration enables people from different backgrounds and skillset to meet each other. During their interaction, they share information, exchange experiences, and form new ways of thinking. Wide collaboration can be achieved by crossing teams, units, departments, functions, and geographies. However, wide collaboration is more than simply "cooperating more with other teams."[20] It requires a shared mission, trust, and understanding of different people's roles in the work involved.

As leaders, here are some ways you can encourage your employees to collaborate more:

- *Build a compelling shared cause*: In psychologist Sherrie Campbell's Entrepreneur article, "10 Simple Ways to Build a Collaborative, Successful Work Environment," she pointed out that team members must be provided with a compelling reason to be part of the company's mission.[21] Give your people a clear mission and they will be as passionate and involved as the leaders are. Refer to "Incorporate Customer Obsession in Your Principles" in this chapter to discover what drives your corporate mission and what problems you are solving for your customers. Share your customer stories with your employees and emphasize the impact of the work that they are doing.

- *Bring people together to solve problems*: Provide your employees with the opportunity to practice working with other people outside their own teams. You can do so by incorporating problem-solving exercises (not just team building but real problems that the organization faces) as part of the talent and leadership development program for participants to work together. During new project formation, try to include employees of different departments to cut across the silos. You can also host hackathons and innovation challenges to offer a collaboration experience. Collaboration behavior will take some time to cultivate. Once employees experience the benefits of collaborating, they will do it more naturally.

- *Create a virtual platform for people to connect*: In large corporations, people usually have lower visibility into what other teams are doing. There might be teams working on a similar initiative, using similar technology, or exploring related concepts but others don't know about it. Without knowing what other teams are up to, it is challenging to keep looking around to find connections blindly. Technology has made it easier today for people to connect despite their location and physical barriers. With a virtual platform, people can connect, share information and best practices, and exchange ideas. Virtual platforms can come in different shapes and forms. I have seen examples such as project portfolios broadcast by teams, regular cross-team sharing sessions, discussion boards, and idea-sharing platforms. Maintaining platforms to ensure robust dynamics requires effort. I have seen good connections formed from some successful platforms. It usually happens in interactive sessions in which people shared what they were doing and other teams discovered connections to their work. On the other hand, I have also seen many examples that failed to serve the purpose and lose traction over time. Reasons for this include lack of up-to-date content or regular maintenance, an unfriendly design with no interaction, and a lack of leadership and diligent execution. If you build a platform for people to connect, make sure you oversee the traffic and follow through with what has to be done to maintain the platform's robustness.

Be Open About Intelligent Failure

The fastest way to succeed is to double your failure rate.

—IBM's Thomas Watson, Sr.

Most leaders and managers do not feel comfortable hearing the word failure. They try their best not to cause any failure in their work and if something happens, it's best not to talk about it. But not all failures are created equal, as Amy C. Edmondson, the Novartis Professor of Leadership at Harvard Business School, discovered. She studied the wisdom of learnings from failures for over 20 years in organizations across industries including pharmaceutical, financial services, product design, telecommunications and construction companies, hospitals, and NASA's space shuttle program.

Edmondson found that for organizations that have not been performing well, their managers look at failures the wrong way. There are millions of things that can go wrong in organizations but the reasons for failure are broadly categorized across a spectrum between blameworthy and praiseworthy.[22] Let's look at the different types of failure and what can be learned from each type.

Failures Due to Mistakes

On the side of blameworthy are failures due to deviance, inattention, lack of ability, and process inadequacy. Most of these failures are considered "bad" failures because in these scenarios there are tightly defined policies, procedures, and processes to prevent them from happening. With proper training and support, employees should be able to follow them consistently. In the case of failure, the cause can be traced, spotted readily, and rectified. With these failures, learnings are continual but limited as they mostly do not involve major breakthroughs.

Unavoidable Failures in Complex Systems

In the middle of the spectrum are failures in complex systems, including task challenges and process complexity. These happen from time to time when there is uncertainty involved in the work, for example, when a new group of team members is put together, a new situation occurs, and new needs from customers arise. These failures are almost like perpetual risks that are unavoidable in complex organizations. They are counterproductive but not necessarily bad.

Intelligent Failures

Toward the other end of the scale are failures due to uncertainty, hypothesis testing, and exploratory testing. Failures in this category are considered "good." These are the failures that offer tremendous learning opportunities and potential growth for the organization. They occur because people are finding new ways of doing things and experimentation is necessary. Experiments come with inherent risk and uncertainty. Every new invention, a new formula, new business model, and new product requires experimentation. With each failure, the innovators are a step closer to the outcome they are looking for, and it is the learnings from those failures that are going to help them achieve success. To innovate, intelligent failures are unavoidable.

Questions for corporate leaders:

- In your organization, what portion of failures falls under blameworthy, unavoidable, or intelligent?
- Has your team been making a good quantity of intelligent failures that enable learnings?

Innovation Accelerates When you Fail Fast, Fail Often

Since intelligent failures are inevitable in the process of innovation due to their experimental nature, the only formula to success is to get through the process systematically and swiftly. If an inventor like Thomas Edison has to experiment with 1,000 lightbulb designs before he finds one that works, he has to experiment faster and more often to figure out the right formula. Instead of being emotionally trapped in the last failure, just pivot and move on. That should also apply to your organization. As a leader, you would want your employees to experiment with a smaller investment, come to a conclusion quickly on what works and what does not, and eventually achieve the innovation breakthrough. Therefore, you should lead your people to think about how they can design experiments smarter and achieve results with fewer resources. In that case, the learnings captured are of quality, quick turnaround time, and low cost.

Leader's Approach to Intelligent Failure

The failure study is often not taken seriously as it is usually emotionally unpleasant for people to look again at their failures. That is why having the right culture is important. You have to create openness for your employees to talk about failure and unlock the learning opportunities. Here are a few notes on how you should approach failure:

- *Analyze the failure*: The next time you see a failure in your corporation, take a closer look and find out what caused it using the spectrum of blameworthy and praiseworthy failures we've just discussed. Instead of being sad or angry about the failure, invite people to discuss what they think went wrong. Listen to their perspectives.
- *Encourage "fail fast, fail often."* If it is an intelligence failure, recognize the effort that the team made to experiment with something new. Congratulate the team on achieving this failure (like an invalidation) using such a small investment. They have de-risked innovation and avoided spending huge effort in the wrong direction. Now that the team has concluded the

last experiment failure, encourage them to pivot and progress
to the next validation.

- *Communicate intelligent failures for others to learn.* Be open
  and transparent about the failure and present it as an opportunity for all to learn. Organizational learnings are valuable
  and sharing them saves other teams' effort and time in their
  experiments. A leader can set the stage by inviting the team
  to share what they have tried that does not work and what the
  team is now moving on to. Emphasize learning and progress.
  By doing so, you will also encourage others to be more open
  to talking about intelligent failures.

Questions for corporate leaders:

- Has there been a recent intelligent failure in the
  organization?
- Has the team done a thorough analysis of the failure?
- Was it an example of "fail fast, fail often"?
- What was the learning?
- How did the team communicate the failure to others?

Reward Innovation

Based on the Incentive Theory of Motivation, incentives are tangible or
intangible rewards that you give to a person based on positive behavior.[23]
By associating a reward with positive behavior, it motivates the person to
continuously repeat the behavior. Rewarding innovation sends a signal to
your employees that this behavior is encouraged and is part of the culture.
However, finding a reward that people view as a good incentive might not
be as straightforward. The concept of reward can also change over time
and in different situations.

Reward Is Not All About Financials

There is no doubt that finance is an important factor at work. Corporations should pay competitive and fair compensation to their employees so

that they can focus on performing their work and not worry about their living. However, beyond that, money does not play such a significant role as we might have expected. In his book *Drive: The Surprising Truth About What Motivates Us*, Daniel H. Pink discovered that the traditional carrot and stick approach—increasing productivity by rewarding good behavior and punishing bad—worked quite well during the Industrial Revolution.[24]

Back then, most of the work was routine based. But as time went by and tasks became more complex and more self-directed, this traditional approach no longer delivered the expected results. In fact, monetary incentives can cause unintended results including unethical behavior, short-term thinking, and so on.[25] It is still important to pay people enough to keep them motivated but, beyond that, people are more motivated by jobs that align with their innate intrinsic motivators:

- *Autonomy*: The desire and need to direct our own lives in terms of time, technique, and task.
- *Mastery*: The need to get better at things and develop further through training and self-improvement.
- *Purpose*: The core human need is to be connected to something bigger than ourselves. The need to do things that matter.

Based on the above principles, you can reward employees in the following ways:

- *Recognition at town hall, conferences, and meetings.* Recognizing the employees has a powerful impact: it makes them feel appreciated. It is the easiest way you can reward employees for the work they have done. Make sure your recognition is specific and timely. Find a way to articulate how the employee's contribution aligned with the mission of your corporation.
- *Grant them the lead role.* If an employee comes up with a brilliant idea, the worst thing you can do is take it away and delegate someone else to drive it. To encourage innovation, assign the person who comes up with the idea as the lead. Let the person drive the idea forward.

- *Include innovation performance in the appraisal.* You can include innovation performance in the performance review and make sure that people managers capture the staff's effort spent on innovation. It then becomes part of the staff profile of the organization and should be considered when it comes to evaluating the opportunities for promotion and mobility.
- *Give them autonomy and flexibility in how they work.* As a leader, your job is to manage the people, not the tasks. Give people a certain degree of autonomy to decide how they want to manage their work. You can start giving autonomy by setting expectations and making people accountable for their own tasks. Your employees will value your trust in them. It also allows them to grow.
- *Give awards, prizes, and perks.* In a global bank I worked for, there is an innovation awards festival every year. Teams working on innovative projects can submit their project description and progress to a central committee. The committee will evaluate the projects, from early to mature-stage projects, and give awards to teams based on specific criteria. To increase participation, employees can also vote for their favorite projects. Announcements of awards are widely publicized internally. Each employee in the awarded team will be granted prize points that they can accumulate to redeem perks in an employee store. Perks include phones, electronic devices, vacations, and so on.

Besides incentives provided by management, there are other official incentives that you can build into your human resource system and policy. For more institutional incentive practices regarding motivating and retaining intrapreneurial talents, refer to Chapter 9.

Reward on a Team Basis

Innovation seldom happens solo. Intrapreneurs might initiate an idea on their own at the start, but to realize the idea, there is usually a team behind them executing it diligently. For that reason, corporations should take a team-based reward approach to encourage collaboration and synergy-building. Fair rewards for team members enhance trust in the team by creating equal opportunity for all to succeed.

Make sure you also reward the people who are involved in moving the idea forward, including risk functions such as legal, compliance, and information security. It demonstrates that the corporation recognizes partners who support innovation. But avoid the pitfall of rewarding too wide a group of people claiming credit. This dilutes the effort made by the real contributing team members.

Reward the Intelligent Failure Too

That might sound strange but if you can reward intelligent failure, you can make impactful progress in building an innovative culture. Look at it this way: by rewarding intelligent failure, you are in fact rewarding the action of "trying." This incentivizes your employees to think outside of conventional ways and create new solutions. Rewarding failure is one of the most powerful ways to eliminate fear. NASA has adopted this by giving employees the "Lean Forward; Fail Smart Award."[26] This award was designed to encourage, recognize, and celebrate the spirit that propels individuals to take the risk to innovate. And while they, unfortunately, failed to reach the desired outcome, they learned from the attempt.

Questions for corporate leaders:

- How do you reward innovation in your organization?
- How can you design a better reward system for innovation?

In this chapter, we have discussed about building a culture that can nurture intrapreneurship. A culture of fear is the number one enemy of intrapreneurship. You can examine whether there is such a culture in your organization by asking yourself the three questions mentioned in this chapter. Then discuss with your management team and employees how they feel about working in your organization.

This chapter has also guided you on the practices required to build a culture for intrapreneurship. Developing a strong customer obsession culture helps shape a team's mindset to create the best value for customers. Building psychological safety is crucial for encouraging employees to challenge the status quo and contribute new ideas. Understand how your management team views failures at the moment and whether you are taking the right approach to handle different types of failures. Use rewards to encourage positive behaviors and it will help you set an example for your people. There are various ways to reward employees mentioned in this chapter that you can implement with your teams.

Setting the right culture is not an overnight process, of course. It takes awareness and a commitment to change. Your culture affects the level of openness of your employees to contribute. But more than that, employees need to be provided with the right tools and processes. In the next chapter, we will talk about the infrastructure you need to build to enable intrapreneurship.

CHAPTER 6

Corporate Infrastructure

Managing innovation and intrapreneurship is not an ad hoc task. It is a disciplined process that requires systematic management. To build sustainable innovation, you need to assemble the infrastructure within your organization to cultivate intrapreneurship. Without the right infrastructure, innovation can be chaotic and hard to manage, as many leaders have told me.

This is why some leaders remain skeptical of intrapreneurship. They are afraid that there is no control over what employees are doing. Having creative people as intrapreneurs means that they require a lot of freedom to explore the unknown and this, they worry, might result in a waste of time. But, in my experience, innovation is only chaotic when there is a lack of discipline. While creativity does require freedom, innovation requires discipline and discipline requires the right infrastructure.

Infrastructure is a very broad term. In the context of this book, corporate infrastructure refers to procedures, protocols, policies, and systems that support intrapreneurship. Sometimes this is given a name, although different corporations use different names. Some call it an intrapreneurship program, some an innovation program, and some have even given it their own branding (e.g., Procter & Gamble's (P&G) GrowthWorks, Citi's D10X^{SM}, and Dupont's "$eed"). Providing the infrastructure for your people to develop themselves as intrapreneurs reinforces the message that they are not navigating the organization alone and that avenues for support are in place.

The starting point for developing an intrapreneurship program is your corporate strategy. The corporate strategy defines the business objectives and sets out how those objectives will be achieved to keep the business ahead of its peers. These are based on the corporation's unique strengths, assets, and competitive advantages, as well as challenges and disruption to the market. The strategy influences all decisions, including business, operations, technology, human resources, and, of course, innovation. You should put together an innovation strategy based on your corporate strategy. An innovation strategy should include five main components:

1. *Why.* The reason for innovating and the vision of the corporation
2. *Who.* The customers you are innovating for
3. *What.* The external forces of change and their influence
4. *How.* The capabilities that the corporation has and is going to build
5. *When.* The frequency of capturing the ideas and the timeline of moving the ideas forward

Let's look at each of these components in turn.

Why. Leaders need to form a vision for innovation. From the vision, you can identify the gap between where you are and where you want to be. It sets a roadmap to the desired future state of the corporation. Seeing the gap gives you a reason why you need to innovate to achieve the envisioned state. This also provides your employees with strong sense of purpose for innovation.

Who. Identify the customer segment that you are innovating for. What are the corporation's competitive advantages today in this segment? What are the customer's unmet needs? For any idea raised by the employees, it should always serve this customer segment by either solving their pain points or discovering new value for them.

What. In the innovation strategy, corporate leaders need to capture the future themes they would like to explore, focus on, and/or invest in. Themes are not specific solutions. Themes could be high-level trends that influence the market dynamics or emerging technologies that might change the competition landscapes. Corporate leaders can brainstorm and lay out themes that they have seen in the market using the following questions:

- What are the trends that are influencing my customers?
- What are the emerging technologies that are relevant to my customers' industry?

- Who could be a new competitor in the future? What enables them?

For example, a corporation in the health care industry might find the following themes relevant:[1]

- Personalization of care
- Virtual care and telehealth
- Agile supply chain
- The Internet of Medical Things ("IoMT")
- Application of data analytics and artificial intelligence
- 5G network
- Augmented, virtual, and mixed reality for health care

All of these themes are influencing the future of the health care industry.

How. What innovation capabilities does the corporation already have? Take an inventory of what you can leverage. What tools can you provide your employees for them to carry out innovation activities? To achieve the vision, what's missing? How do you plan to acquire those capabilities?

Using the innovation strategy, you can create a system of strategic intrapreneurship with a specific focus. As Professor Bulent Güven described in his article "The Integration of Strategic Management and Intrapreneurship,"[2] strategic intrapreneurship is the process of promoting innovation and creating policies according to the organization's competitive advantages and core competencies. It enables employees to turn discoveries and opportunities into advantages.

You should widely discuss the innovation strategy with employees to keep them informed and inspire them to explore the possibilities. Broadcasting the innovation strategy can make them feel involved and engaged. Sharing the areas of focus allows employees who aspire to become intrapreneurs to understand where they should invest their efforts. They can then prioritize problems or solutions that are better aligned with the corporate strategy.

When. Innovation is not a one-off exercise. The timeliness of capturing and moving ideas forward is crucial to the success of your organization. Imagine if you review ideas only once a year and so happen that an employee with a brilliant idea missed the round. The idea might be brought to you a year later but the opportunity might have been missed. Even worse, the employee might have left your organization and brought the idea to another company.

To manage the timeliness of innovation, you need to decide the appropriate frequency of reviewing the following five areas:

1. Idea capturing
   Ideally, idea submission should be open at all times. Some organizations manage the idea capturing by hosting events or campaigns. With that, idea capturing is more dependent on the occasional events and the cost of capturing ideas also increases.

2. Ideas funding
   To create a robust pipeline of innovative projects, you need to review and fund ideas promptly. A quarterly review is a good basis to start with. If this is done less than two times a year, you would be at risk of losing competitiveness and time to market.

3. Progress of funded ideas
   Once the idea is funded, a regular review of the progress is required. This is to ensure that the project is moving forward. If the project is not progressing as expected, the review would provide the opportunity for the founder team to escalate the roadblocks and seek support to clear them. A monthly review would be a good frequency to start.

4. Innovation management
   Leaders should review the efficiency of the innovation management, preferably every six months. This is to evaluate whether the approach leads to the desired results or target of innovation.

5. Innovation strategy
   Changes across the various industries have been accelerated. Corporations are facing rapid disruptions. The innovation trends that your team has identified at the beginning of the year might not be relevant at the end of the year. The competition might have changed. Therefore, a yearly review is required to understand the landscape that your corporation is in.

Questions for corporate leaders:

- Do you have an innovation strategy?
- How does the innovation strategy align with your corporate strategy?
- What are the key trends in your industry?
- How often do you review the way you approach innovation and intrapreneurship?

Idea Management

In the daily interaction in a corporation, too many good ideas are left unspoken or raised but lost. Ideas need to be managed in a systematic and structured way to give you visibility of the idea pool and its potential.

Idea Funnel

To better manage the ideas in the corporation, you need a mechanism, the *idea funnel,* to generate, capture, assess, and track the progress of ideas. The idea funnel provides you with the opportunity to:

- *Generate new ideas in the organization.* Using events like hack-athon, innovation workshops, or bootcamps, corporates can lead employees' engagement to generate ideas to solve specific problems. The ideas are outcomes of the event and will be captured in the idea funnel. The funnel also acts as the pool to capture ideas coming from all sources in the corporation.
- *Gain visibility of ideas across silos.* Once the ideas are captured in a pool, people from various departments and teams can view the ideas, see where the ideas sit, who the founders are, what problems they are trying to solve, what themes they fall under, and so on.
- *Build synergies among similar ideas.* With the visibility of other ideas in the corporation, corporate leaders or employees can reach out to build on each other's ideas. This is particularly

important in a large organization as typically teams are working on similar ideas or ideas that leverage similar technologies. The sharing of learnings and building collaboration can help the team to expedite the innovation process and avoid overlapping efforts.

- *Evaluate ideas easily.* Having the ideas in one place allows leaders and relevant stakeholders to discuss and evaluate ideas on the same platform. It also provides a good track record of decisions made, who made them, and the rationale behind them. Plus, it helps build up the corporate knowledge of idea decision making.

- *Increase transparency of progress.* Mostly after ideas are sponsored, progress-tracking relies on the project team themselves and it is made visible to the close stakeholders. It also depends on the proactiveness of the team members to update their progress. Having a tracking system in place requires the team to report the progress, at least on a high-level basis, in the funnel. This information is important for leaders. You have to be aware of the innovations that you expect to be launched in the near term and form the strategy accordingly.

To manage the idea funnel efficiently, you can deploy idea management software out of the box, customize an existing offering, or build a proprietary one. Mature idea management software includes Agorize, BrightIdea, IdeaDrop, and Viima. In a corporate that I worked with previously, the idea management software was developed in-house. It was a small build and launching it took around six weeks. Depending on how tailored you want the software to be and the available resources, a build versus buy analysis will help you decide how you deploy the idea management software.

The scope of a basic idea management software includes:

- Capture idea: founder(s), sponsor(s), department, relevant product, theme, date, potential impact (revenue/cost saving), or any other information required by the management.
- Capture keywords of an idea to identify similar ideas.

- Evaluate idea: reviewer's input, decision vote: approve/reject/ more validation needed, justification field.
- Progress tracking by stage: ideation, prototype, proof of concept, solution launch, and scale.
- Web access is simplest, compared to an application or software being installed.

Idea Evaluation Framework

To guide the evaluation of ideas, you will need to develop a framework. It is an agreed list of lenses and criteria that apply to all ideas submitted. The framework guides which ideas should be approved or sponsored to proceed to the next stage. Without a framework, the stakeholders would likely rely on their instincts to assess the idea and lose objectivity. Once you have the framework in place, communicate it to your employees and make it transparent. That can help them in their innovation process as they can conduct self-assessment and prepare accordingly when they put up an idea.

An idea evaluation framework should capture all the key criteria that are used to evaluate the idea. A good framework should be comprehensive and help review ideas through the lenses of design thinking, solution readiness, and alignment with the corporate innovation strategy. Yet it has to be simple enough and not so intimidating that it deters people from submitting an idea.

Here are some criteria that you can consider putting into the framework. For each of the points below, you can apply a scale of 1 (lowest) to 5 (highest) for the evaluation team to provide their scoring individually.

1. *Customer centricity.* How does the idea address a key customer problem statement? To what extent does the customer want this problem solved?
2. *Killer idea.* How well does the idea address a key customer pain point? Is this a painkiller or a vitamin solution?
3. *Technology capability.* How mature is the required technology for building the idea?

4. *Innovation alignment.* To what extent does the idea align with the innovation strategy and the focus areas?

5. *Unique value proposition.* To what extent does the idea differentiate your corporation from competitors and provide a unique competitive advantage?

6. *Proprietary assets.* To what extent does the idea leverage the corporate advantages of the core businesses?

7. *Commercial viability.* How big is the opportunity (in revenue or cost saving) for the corporate?

8. *Speed to market.* How long would it take to launch the solution?

9. *Scalability.* To what extent could the idea scale across the markets in which the corporation operates?

Figure 6.1 is a template of the idea evaluation criteria. Each organization is unique in terms of its desired goal of innovation, and the criteria can be tailored to fit your corporate strategy.

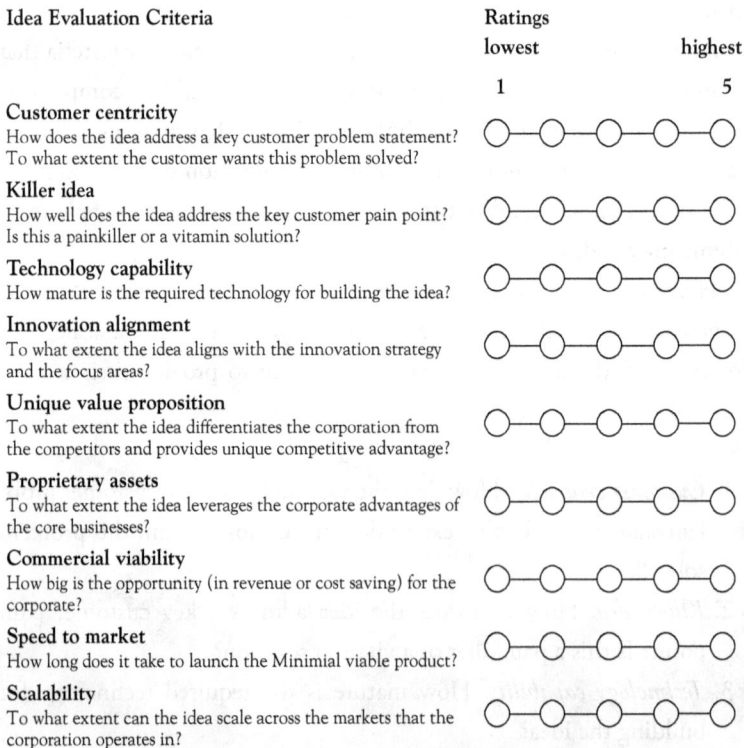

Idea Evaluation Criteria	Ratings	
	lowest	highest
	1	5
Customer centricity How does the idea address a key customer problem statement? To what extent the customer wants this problem solved?	O—O—O—O—O	
Killer idea How well does the idea address the key customer pain point? Is this a painkiller or a vitamin solution?	O—O—O—O—O	
Technology capability How mature is the required technology for building the idea?	O—O—O—O—O	
Innovation alignment To what extent the idea aligns with the innovation strategy and the focus areas?	O—O—O—O—O	
Unique value proposition To what extent the idea differentiates the corporation from the competitors and provides unique competitive advantage?	O—O—O—O—O	
Proprietary assets To what extent the idea leverages the corporate advantages of the core businesses?	O—O—O—O—O	
Commercial viability How big is the opportunity (in revenue or cost saving) for the corporate?	O—O—O—O—O	
Speed to market How long does it take to launch the Minimial viable product?	O—O—O—O—O	
Scalability To what extent can the idea scale across the markets that the corporation operates in?	O—O—O—O—O	

Figure 6.1 Idea evaluation criteria template

The framework would help the team that evaluates the ideas to break down the analysis from a different perspective. These scores provide an estimate. However, the analysis should not be simply about approving the ideas with the highest scores. The shortfall of the scoring is that it might not be able to capture the entire picture of the idea and sometimes it is too subjective. As a best practice, an evaluation panel should be formed and each member should submit their scoring (including total scores and the breakdown). A deliberation session should then be hosted. All the scores would be shown as references and there should be a time-bound discussion on each idea. Based on the point of view of the panel, they should collectively agree on the ideas to proceed with. Sometimes the best idea might seem difficult to digest. A diverse group on the panel helps when it comes to understanding the opportunity presented. That's why deliberation is very important on top of the actual score.

Idea Evaluation Panel

It is best practice to have diverse representatives on the panel to consider all aspects of the idea. You should always strive to have a panel instead of an individual deciding on new ideas. That can avoid individual biases limited by one individual's experience or mindset. Having a panel gives the process credibility. Employees will feel that their ideas are taken seriously and not controlled by one person alone.

The next question is: who should sit on the panel? To form a strong panel, you need people who are senior enough to sponsor ideas, people who understand customers, people who understand the implications for the business, people who can contribute their subject expertise, and people who can view ideas from an entrepreneurial perspective. A good panel would consist of a team with:

1. *Senior sponsor*: A highly influential leader who is powerful enough to sponsor the idea. This person sees the strategic direction of the company and helps support the idea using their influence.
2. *Business or sales head*: A leader who is overseeing the profit and loss (P&L) of the business or a leader with a strong understanding of customers' needs. This person can evaluate the opportunity from a commercial angle.

3. *Technology head*: A leader who is overseeing the technology capability and architecture. This person can evaluate the relevant technical requirements and see whether there is any existing capability that the idea can leverage.

4. *Subject matter expert*: A specialist who is experienced in the field to which the idea is relevant. The specialist would have a thorough understanding of the existing process and can give their opinion on whether the idea is solving the right problem.

5. *Innovation lead/entrepreneur in residence*: Someone who can view the idea from an outsider's perspective and provide entrepreneurial input. It could be a person who is hired to innovate or someone who has been an entrepreneur. This person would provide input based on their experience of innovation or building a new business.

6. *Customer community (optional)*: What could be better than getting direct feedback from your customers? If possible, having a customer community or representative on your idea evaluation panel would bring tremendous value. With real customers involved, the team no longer has to "guess" whether the customers are receptive to the idea.

Figure 6.2 shows the key personnel to be included in the idea evaluation panel.

Depending on the different types of ideas and the associated products, you can bring in other relevant stakeholders to the evaluation panel. However, do note that the optimal panel is a nimble one. The more people you have, the more group think could occur. The decision process would be slowed down because too much agreement is required.

If the idea pipeline is robust, you can consider having decentralized idea evaluation panels instead of a single team to consider them. Having

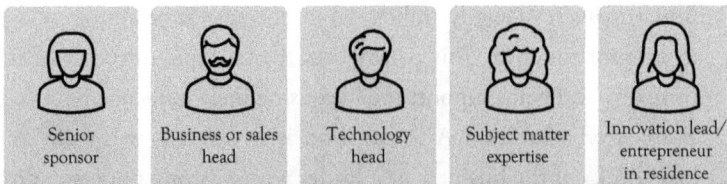

Figure 6.2 Idea evaluation panel

multiple idea evaluation panels means that evaluation takes place more frequently and this speeds up decision making. As you can imagine, if ideas are only evaluated on a half-yearly or quarterly basis, you might miss a window of opportunity to get the idea sponsored. The panels could be organized along business lines or geography, and different ideas could be allocated to different panels.

What Does Sponsorship Mean?

Before you fire the starting gun and ask people to pitch ideas, you must answer one major question: what does sponsorship mean? Employees who pitch ideas want to know what it will mean for them if their pitch is successful. I have seen situations in which the sponsorship was not well defined or there was little commitment from the organization. The intrapreneurs in these cases became disappointed and frustrated and eventually walked away from the idea they were once passionate about.

I urge you to think through the commitment you want to make for innovation to thrive. If the ideas are worth your sponsorship, what kind of support are you willing to provide to your intrapreneurs? Consider all of the following commitments:

- *Time investment.* Do you expect intrapreneurs to work extra hours on top of their day jobs to push the idea forward? Naturally, intrapreneurs would be driven to do so. Building a new idea can be an intensive task, especially once it gets through the initial ideation stage. Expecting intrapreneurs to work full-time as well as build a new business might not be entirely realistic or sustainable. It might cost the corporation with the intrapreneur either not handling their original job well or not making good progress on the new idea. On the other hand, it might not be practical to invite the intrapreneur to walk away from their day job and focus solely on their new idea. It is too risky for both the corporation and the employee. When employees are asked whether they would opt to become full-time intrapreneurs, most of them are skeptical when an idea is at an early stage as it lacks job security. Consider providing a commitment to a percentage of time you want the intrapreneurs to work on the idea. 3M uses the 15 percent rule to invite its employees to devote about 15 percent of their time to experimental doodling or work on self-initiated projects.[3] Alphabet, the parent company of Google, applies a "20-percent time rule" for projects that would benefit Google.[4] If you interpret the percentage of time during a workweek, 20 percent is one in five workdays. So Google is allowing employees to use one day per week to explore and work on their own ideas.

- *Seed funding*. For intrapreneurs to proceed with discovery and development, there are often resources required. Consider providing a small amount of funding for the ideas that successfully obtained sponsorship. To support the new ideas, set aside a pool of funding that people can bid for each year. There should be strict rules and accounting for the funding usage, for example, for research, product development, or technology capability relevant only to the idea raised. Consider providing the grants in a staged manner so there is lower risk associated with investing too much upfront. Refer to "Innovation pipeline management" in this chapter for more information about managing ideas through different stages.

- *Mentorship*. Intrapreneurs require extensive support to move things forward. Assigning mentors who are subject matter experts or senior management can help them navigate and expedite the process. Having a highly influential leader as a mentor or advisor on the team can help open doors for them and foster collaboration across various functions. Communicate clearly with mentors, setting expectations for their roles and responsibilities.

Whatever commitment you have decided upon and broadcast to your organization, do stick to it. You might not see change overnight or new products invented in three months. It will take time for employees to test the water, observe examples, and build faith in the new system.

Intrapreneurship in Action: The LinkedIn [in]cubator—Managing New Ideas

LinkedIn has run an intrapreneurship program since 2012.[5] Once a quarter, any LinkedIn employee can come up with an idea, put together a team, and pitch their project to the executive staff. If approved, the team gets to spend up to three months of dedicated time turning their ideas into reality.

Before the concept of [in]cubator was formed, LinkedIn practiced intrapreneurship through an initiative called Hackday. Hackday is a Friday each month when employees are encouraged to work on just about anything they want. In his article "The LinkedIn [in]cubator," the SVP of Engineering Kevin Scott recalled that although there were incredible ideas and prototypes during Hackday, there's a natural limit to what can be achieved in one day. With LinkedIn [in]cubator, ideas could be taken to the next level. The teams who performed best during Hackday could further pitch the idea to the executive, get approval, and pilot the idea. To increase senior sponsorship, the executive panel that would assess ideas included CEO Jeff Weiner, cofounder Reid Hoffman, and SVP of Products and User Experience Deep Nishar, as well as Kevin Scott.

Scott thinks of [in]cubator projects as small investments with the potential to become big wins for the company. With every approval of a project, the executive panel also signs up as advisors for the team. They meet with approved teams weekly to give guidance and do everything they can to make them successful.

Ideas That Might Self-Cannibalize

When you open the funnel to capture ideas, there'll often be some ideas that could cannibalize your old business. As an example, let's consider a travel agency that earns most of its income from booking air tickets for customers over the phone. Customers call the agency's staff, who check ticket availability for them. The turnaround time is long and the commission fee is opaque. With the new technology available today, there's bound to be a better way of doing things.

The idea for a digital self-service system comes from an intrapreneur, who suggests that customers could go to the agency's website. There, they could check all air tickets online and book in real time. For the sake of this example, let's assume that no competitor (like Expedia) has launched before and, if the corporation pursues it, it might be the first to market.

What are the pros and cons? Well, the commission on digital booking could potentially be lower as the cost of operation is lower than the phone system. The customer experience would definitely be better, given the quicker response and seamless checkout. However, the idea would certainly cannibalize the current phone-based business and affect profitability, since that existing department is the company's bread and butter. What should you do?

Cannibalization sounds scary. Many corporations are skeptical about launching new products because they might impact existing ones. However, while in the short term this might work to protect existing profitability, in the long run, it is going to endanger the company's survival.

If you don't cannibalize yourself, someone else will.

—Steve Jobs

It might seem ideal if you can stop the new idea from eating your existing lunch. However, you are only able to stop those within your company. In the external world, your competitors and other startups are innovating relentlessly to seize market share. It is only a matter of time before they launch the innovation that you did not.

The recommended approach is to embrace cannibalization.[6] However, that's more easily said than done as it feels unnatural to replace a profitable business. The key is to focus on what customers really need (refer to "Create a culture with strong customer obsession" in Chapter 5), evaluate the impact of cannibalization and the time taken to launch and scale up the new product, and make a decision and move forward.

> Questions for corporate leaders:
>
> - How do you capture ideas in your organization today?
> - Do you have a framework for idea evaluation?

Innovation Pipeline Management

Capturing and evaluating ideas are great starting points. But ideas remain ideas until they are developed and implemented. To help your intrapreneurs make progress, you need to have a system, the pipeline funnel, to progress the idea.

The innovation pipeline funnel is used to manage sponsored ideas. There are multiple stages within the funnel and each stage has associated inputs and outputs. The stages include discovery, proof of concept, minimal viable product (MVP) launch, and scale-up. Figure 6.3 illustrates how an idea flows through the innovation pipeline funnel.

1. *Discovery.* After the idea has been sponsored, the team needs to do more discovery work on the problem and solution exploration. Refer to Chapter 7, "Problem-Solving by Design Thinking," under "Disciplined Innovation" for more information about the process. At this stage, the team needs to assess whether the idea has legs. It also requires the team to form a well-crafted concept to explain how the idea works from end to end. Some prototyping will happen during this stage to experiment with the design of the product and to test customer receptiveness.

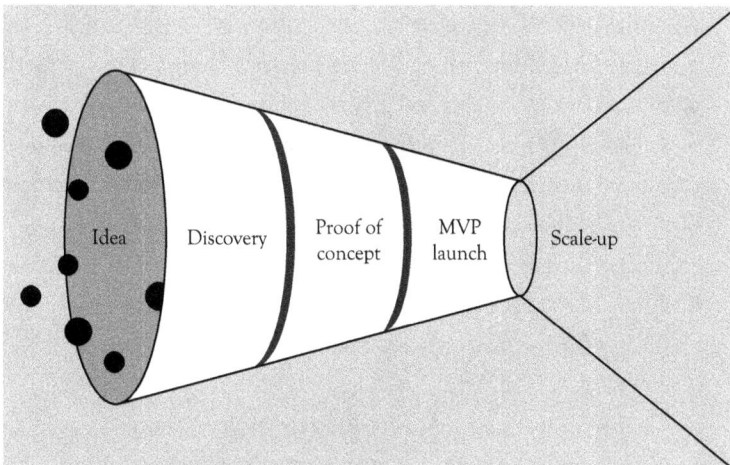

Figure 6.3 Innovation pipeline funnel

Key inputs: Problem statement, hypothesis, high-level idea

Key activities: Research, customer interviews, crafting of solution concept, crafting business model canvas

Key outputs: Validated problem statement or hypothesis, design of solution concept, high-level business model, target customers

2. *Proof of concept.* With the solution concept crafted, the team has to prove that the concept actually works. They can break the concept down into various experiments to test the components before they assemble the solution.

Key inputs: Design of solution concept

Key activities: Design of experiment, testing via experiments, iteration of experiments

Key outputs: Proof-of-concept results, validated or invalidated solution concept

3. *MVP launch.* After the team confirms that the solution can be built, they need to decide on the key features to include in the first version of the product. This requires them to form an MVP that can deliver the desired function and experience to the customer without excessive build. Some refer to this stage as the pilot stage.

Key inputs: Validated solution concept, high-level business model, target customers

Key activities: Defining MVP, developing the MVP, finalizing business model, design of production services, go-to-market

Key outputs: MVP delivered to target customer

4. *Scale-up.* Depending on the feedback from the MVP launch, the team might go through a few pivots of launches before they move on to the scale-up stage. Pivoting is required when the team discovers that a major direction change is needed to achieve success. Examples of pivots include:

- Change in key solution features
- Change in targeted customers
- Change in the platform, for example, an application or software
- Change in business model to increase monetization
- Change in technology to lower cost or create a more robust product

By learning from pivots, the team gets a better understanding of what a successful product looks like and is in a better position to replicate it across different markets and customer segments.

Key inputs: MVP or pivoted MVPs, customer feedback, product, market roadmap

Key activities: Planning for the scale-up, forming long-term strategy, transitioning pilot to expansion

Key outputs: Scaled solution across markets or customer segments

The time taken to proceed from one stage to another varies and it might not necessarily be a linear process. If the team has done sufficient work before the pitch, some activities might have already been catered for during the early stage and they can skip ahead. The main purpose of having a funnel is to help the team expedite the process by visualizing the innovation activities and understanding the checkpoints. The skills required to navigate the process are covered in more depth in Chapter 7, "Essential Skills of Intrapreneurship."

The Pause, Pivot, or Kill Switch

Not all ideas can proceed through the stages and finally come to scale. The pausing and termination of an idea or project is also part of innovation pipeline management. Corporations have finite resources to invest in new ideas. There is an opportunity cost if you linger on ideas that have a low chance to succeed and keep deploying resources (be it money or person-hours) on them. At each stage of the funnel, validation is required for the idea to proceed to the next stage. Ideas that fail the validation in a time-bound period should be put on hold until new findings are available, pivoted for new tests, or even dropped. If you observe below, consider pressing the switch at the end of each stage before the project proceeds to the next stage:

1. *Discovery*
   - There is no articulated problem statement or opportunity area.
   - The hypothesis is not validated.
   - The target customers are unclear.

2. *Proof of concept*
   - The solution has not been proved technically feasible.
   - The design of the solution does not create a good customer experience.
   - The proposed business model is unclear.
3. *MVP*
   - The business model has been proven not viable.
   - The pilot result is not satisfactory (depends on the success criteria set for the pilot).
   - The customer feedback is negative.

This list is a general reference for determining whether a project should move forward. Usually, for each project, there are unique assumptions at each stage that the team would seek to validate. Discussing the pause, pivot, or kill mechanism upfront and having a clear mechanism can help increase transparency and provide strong motivation to the founder team.

Upon Scaling Up

When an innovation project moves toward the right end of the funnel and scale-up, the leader will have a decision to make: what is the long-term strategic plan for this project? You should always consider including this discussion when the project moves along the funnel, not toward the very end of it. In that way, both the founder team and the relevant stakeholders can have time to plan the relevant deployment or handover if required. Toward the right side of the funnel, this discussion is much more needed and enriched as the project has a higher chance of success.

Asking about the long-term strategic plan allows the leader and the project team to think through:

- What role does this new solution play in this organization in a long run?
- Where should it sit within this organization?
- Who should be managing it in a long run?
- What is the roadmap for this solution?

There are several ways that the corporate can handle the new solution upon scaling up:

1. Absorbing the new solution into an existing product line
   In this case, the new solution launched is adjacent to an existing product line and shares similar operating characteristics, including factors that influence sales and profit, talents required, and business model. There is an existing product team that excels at expanding the rollout of launched solutions and maintaining the product at scale. It would be best to integrate this new solution into the existing product line.

   The founder team should be given a choice to become the product manager of this new solution, reporting to the management of the existing product line.

2. Create a new product line
   In this case, the new solution launched demonstrates distinctively different characteristics from any existing product of the corporate. It is not quite suitable to manage the solution under any existing product line. However, the corporate sees the potential of a new product line being formed. The management also believes that this new product line would become a strategic initiative that is crucial to the corporate's development in the future.

   The founder team should be offered leadership positions for this new product line. The management might need to hire or transfer people to assist or lead along with the founder team, depending on the business opportunity.

3. Spin-off the project into a new company
   In this case, the new solution launched also demonstrates distinctively different characteristics from any existing product. More than that, the management believes that it is not the best fit for the new solution to be managed as part of its business. There are several potential reasons:
   • Commercial independency: The new solution might be relevant to other industry players and would perform better if this solution is commercially independent.

- Consortium: The new solution is solving a problem that requires collaboration from other players and the corporate alone does not have sufficient effort to further scale it. Other players should be invited to the table and form a consortium.
- Strategic alignment: The new solution does not demonstrate strategic significance to the corporate in a long run. This concern should be eliminated before scaling the solution. However, it is understood that potential management or strategy change could result in relevant change along the funnel.
- ROI (return on investment) of corporate investment: The ROI of a startup, funded by venture capitalists, justifies its development but the ROI of putting it under the existing corporate business does not. It would be rather uncommon in this situation, as usually the cost of capital for corporate would be lower than those of venture capitalists. However, there could be exceptions due to the nature of the industry, the type of project, or the accounting rules.

The new solution will be spun off into a new company. In most cases, the corporate would continue to hold a minority stake in this new company and enjoy the return of investment as a reward.

This new company would be run independently. The founder team should be invited to assume the leadership positions of this new company. The team would no longer be an employee of the existing corporate.

Intrapreneurship in Action: BASF Spun Off Employee Startup BOXLAB

BASF, one of the largest German multinational chemical companies, has been hosting its internal business incubator, Chemovator, since 2019. The incubator has been set up to support its employees to validate ideas. It is promoted as a protected space for BASF intrapreneurs.

Mischa has been working with BASF for 17 years. As a process manager in the Agricultural division, he has observed a problem:

There is a lack of an efficient way to replace damaged packaging and labels in the chemistry industry. He teamed up with Lisa Raschke, a former teammate, to tackle this problem as they believed this process should be improved. They wanted to build a scalable and sustainable solution to optimize the label and packaging process.

They pitched their idea to Chemovator and became a venture team of this incubator. Within 1.5 years, with the support of the Chemovator, they have developed an app BOXLAB that replaces the damaged packaging and label in a fast and easy manner. BOXLAB helped improve the supply chain processes which reduced waste and cost. They have also attracted interest from other chemistry players and forwarding companies who want to improve their supply chain and become more sustainable.

Since the problem that BOXLAB solved was not a standalone problem of BASF, it makes more sense to commercialize it by selling it to other companies who find it relevant. BASF decided to spin off this internal startup. BOXLAB became the first spin-off of BASF coming out from Chemovator and BASF continued to hold a minority stake in the BOXLAB. Both Mischa and Lisa became the managing directors of this new venture BOXLAB Services GmbH.

Question for corporate leaders:

How do you manage innovation pipelines today?

Innovation Portfolio Management

Not every innovation is created equal. Innovation is a very broad term and optimizing a workflow is very different from introducing a brand-new business model, as is the potential risk and return associated with each one. That's why you need to look at your current innovation portfolio and review whether the investment aligns well with the corporate and innovation strategy. Is the investment directed in the best way to generate the outcome set out in the corporate vision?

As an example, let's say that an automobile company aspires to be the leader in autonomous driving. All its current innovation projects focus only on increasing efficiency in the production line. There is no project or any planned investment in IoT and artificial intelligence (AI), which enable autonomous driving. It is obvious that there is a gap in the innovation portfolio.

In most cases, the gap won't be so obvious. That's why you need a structured innovation portfolio management framework to show you what innovations the corporation is investing in and where the gaps are. A framework for managing an innovation portfolio is the Innovation Ambition Matrix.[7]

The Innovation Ambition Matrix was developed by Bansi Nagji and Geoff Tuff. In the *Harvard Business Review* article "Managing Your Innovation Portfolio," they discussed how corporations should manage innovation strategically by categorizing different activities.[8] They discovered that companies with the strongest innovation track record not only had a clear innovation ambition, but also struck the right balance of core, adjacent, and transformational initiatives across the enterprise.

- *Core innovation*: Optimizing existing products for existing customers, for example, small upgrades of existing product offerings, launching updates to keep up with regulatory change, and new packaging design.
- *Adjacent innovation*: Expanding from existing business into "new to the company" business, for example, introducing a new product with a different value proposition for entering a new market.
- *Transformational innovation*: Developing breakthroughs and inventing things for markets that don't yet exist.

To illustrate how the three types of innovation are categorized under the Innovation Ambition Matrix, here are some examples of Coca-Cola's latest innovation activities.

Core Innovation: Orange Vanilla Coke[9, 10, 11]

Coke is the classic signature drink that Coca-Cola has in its product line. However, there is always intense competition from other soft drink brands. To encourage existing customers who are seeking more variety to stick with Coke rather than pick up a different soda, Coca-Cola constantly launches new flavors like Orange Vanilla, which was introduced to the market in early 2019. Kate Carpenter, brand director for Coca-Cola Trademark, said that the new flavor also comes with new graphics for a "bit of a facelift."

Orange vanilla-flavored Coke is considered a core innovation, introducing a slightly new element to an existing product for existing customers. In the first quarter of 2019, Coca-Cola reported 6 percent retail value growth in its flagship markets, thanks to the strong performance of both Coke Zero Sugar and new flavor combinations including Orange Vanilla Coke.

Adjacent Innovation: Coca-Cola Energy[12, 13]

In general, anyone can be a target customer of a soft drink brand. But if you look closer, there are particular types of people portrayed in Coca-Cola's advertisements. The three particular personas that Coca-Cola has been targeting are progressive people, people who have fun and enjoy every minute, and people with stylish looks.[14] Using these personas, Coca-Cola has successfully captured an audience of young, active, and social people. And Coke has been selling well to these groups.

However, Coca-Cola realized that the personas they target do not cover a large market of the working class: the type of people who are always busy. They don't just work from 9 to 5 and call it a day. Their lives are full, and they're doing so many more things after "work." They have a lot of work and little fun time. Their need for a drink is to take in energy instead of enjoying themselves. They are not the typical customers of Coca-Cola beverages as they'd prefer an energy drink to a Coke. But at the same time, they do not really fancy most energy drinks in the market as the taste is usually not good.

Coca-Cola identified this gap and the unmet needs of this customer segment. It launched a Coke-branded energy drink in 2020 to offer the kick people wanted with the Coke taste they were familiar with. The Coke-branded energy drink is an adjacent innovation as Coca-Cola was using this new product to venture into an energy drink market dominated by companies like Red Bull GmbH and Monster Beverage Co.

However, sales were disappointing. At the end of 2020, Coca-Cola Energy represented just 0.7 percent of U.S. energy drink sales, according to *Beverage Digest*. The failure of this innovation could be attributed partly to COVID-19.[15] The product entered the U.S. market in January 2020, but the pandemic soon interrupted its rollout. When people are working from home and paying fewer visits to stores, they tend to order products they have tried before.

Coca-Cola constantly evaluates the performance of its innovation and since the sales of Coca-Cola Energy were not satisfactory, it decided to discontinue Coca-Cola Energy in the United States. During this period, two other adjacent innovations, Coca-Cola with Coffee and AHA-flavored sparkling water, performed well and the company continued selling them.

Transformational Innovation: Direct to Consumers[16]

Both the core and adjacent innovation examples above were initiated by Coca-Cola by listening to their customers and understanding their preferences. These innovation activities affected the flavors and features of the beverages. But innovation initiatives of Coca-Cola go further. Coca-Cola is a global business that sells via local communities. Its products are sold in more than 200 countries. But Coca-Cola does not fill all the bottles or own all the retail outlets. To get its products to local supermarkets and stores, many intermediaries are involved. There are approximately 225 bottling partners worldwide, to which Coca-Cola sends its concentrates. The bottled beverages then go through the distribution system of wholesalers, who help sell the beverages to supermarkets, stores, restaurants, or e-commerce retailers. The system has worked well and provided the scale that Coca-Cola needs to serve millions of customers around the world.

Many companies, which operate in the consumer goods space, rely on similar distribution systems with many wholesalers as intermediaries. However, the system has its problems:

- *Lower profit margin.* Intermediaries earn profit as middlemen, which means part of Coca-Cola's profit is shared with them.

- *Slow to market.* On average, a new product launch takes between 18 and 36 months from the point of inception to the point when the product reaches the shop floor.[17]
- *Inconsistent customer experience.* Coca-Cola has no control over the customer experience. It does not own any last-mile touchpoint so it cannot guarantee a consistent experience from order to consumption.
- *Lack of data control.* Coca-Cola only has access to limited data captured from its distribution system. It can get sales data but not any of the precious data about customers' preferences, behaviors, and feedback.

Given that, manufacturers and consumer goods companies are rethinking their business models to go direct to consumers and eliminate the intermediaries. Yet the uncertainty of this innovation is high as it requires extensive digital and logistics infrastructure and might risk the existing relationship with wholesalers.

In 2020, the COVID-19 lockdowns in Latin America put tremendous pressure on all retailers, particularly small, independently operated stores in high-density urban areas that depended almost solely on foot traffic. Coca-Cola viewed it as an opportunity to test the direct-to-consumer model. At its Coca-Cola Argentina initiative, it developed and launched the Wabi app for small businesses to receive proximity orders, sell their products (not just soft drinks), and take them home.[18]

The Wabi app allowed operators to stay open during the pandemic and safely serve customers without having to be physically open. When a shopper placed an order via a free mobile app, the platform pinged nearby retailers. The first store to accept the order delivered the items to the shopper's doorstep in 30 minutes or less.

The Wabi app is considered a transformational innovation. Coca-Cola anticipated the needs of consumers during the lockdown and disrupted the traditional wholesaler system that it previously relied on for distribution. Wabi went live in 23 major cities across five continents, connecting Coca-Cola's system and other consumer products companies to store owners and end-users.

Finding the Right Balance

Once you understand the types of innovation, you can put your existing portfolios into different categories to evaluate them. The next question you have to ask is, "Do I have the right balance of different types of innovation that will allow me to achieve my corporate vision?"

Depending on the maturity of the corporation's business and the corporate strategy, you need to allocate investment to different categories of innovation. But this can be difficult in large, established corporations. When there are many established assets, including products, markets, and processes, it's hard for people to think outside the box. Coupled with a tendency toward risk avoidance, many ideas that are generated and approved eventually fall under core or slightly adjacent innovation. Transformational innovation, therefore, becomes rare.

To find the right balance in an innovation portfolio, Bansi Nagji and Geoff Tuff studied the industrial, technology, and consumer goods sectors. They looked at whether any particular allocation of resources across different types of innovation initiatives correlated with significantly better performance, as reflected in the share price. They discovered that companies that allocated about 70 percent of their innovation activity to core initiatives, 20 percent to adjacent ones, and 10 percent to transformational ones outperformed their peers. They typically realized a price to earnings (P/E) premium of 10 to 20 percent. To what extent did different types of innovation generate income? They consistently found that the return ratio was roughly the inverse of the resource allocation. Core innovation typically contributed 10 percent of the long-term, cumulative return on innovation investment. Adjacent initiatives contributed 20 percent, and transformational efforts contributed 70 percent.

Of course, these are average figures and do not mean that this allocation is a magic number for all. Each company is unique, with its own competitive advantage and assets. You should consider your investment in different innovation activities based on your corporate vision and innovation strategy. While that varies from corporation to corporation, it is recommended that you constantly manage your innovation portfolio and review your investment allocation.

> Question for corporate leaders:
>
> Do you have a good mix of core, adjacent, and transformational innovation in your organization?

IT Infrastructure

A craftsman who wishes to practice his craft well must first sharpen his tools.

—Confucius

Intrapreneurship is built on an experimental approach. To enable your employees to conduct experiments, leaders have to put in place an intrapreneur-friendly IT infrastructure. IT infrastructure refers to the hardware, software, networks, facilities, and equipment used to develop, test, monitor, control, or support IT services.[19] Examples of IT infrastructure include data centers, communication networks, IT security, and end-user technology services. In this section, we will focus on infrastructure related to innovation under Industry 5.0. Even though not all innovation is related to IT services, during the development of a new product there is a high chance that intrapreneurs would use components of IT infrastructure to perform some of the tasks.

If a corporation relies on its legacy infrastructure and applies the same infrastructure across its production and experimental environment, it will find it hard to catch up with the pace of innovation. It also runs the risk of operational failure. That's why many see existing IT infrastructure as a roadblock to innovation.

An IT infrastructure that truly supports innovation should aim at empowering all employees to become innovators. To enable an experimental environment, corporations need an agile, scalable IT infrastructure. It should allow experiments in a safe environment with rapid setup, flexible scalability, and compatibility with modern and emerging technologies, for example AI, blockchain, and IoT.

IT infrastructure that you need to support intrapreneurship in your organization should be:

- *Agile.* Designed to support the rapid development and launch of MVPs, incremental upgrades, and improvements
- *Scalable.* Launch, grow, recede, or terminate based on the demands of traffic and volume of users
- *Isolatable.* Allows experiments in isolation without risking harm to the production environment
- *Accessible.* Provide easy access for employees to explore the resources and initiate experiments on their own
- *Integratable.* Connects the delivery of new solutions to the legacy system and is highly compatible with emerging technologies
- *Secure.* Protected from hacks and unauthorized access
- *Cost-effective.* An IT infrastructure that does not require huge, multiyear upfront investment to set up and maintain

In the Industry 5.0 environment, you need to plan and deploy relevant IT infrastructure that aligns with your innovation strategy. It's an investment to enable innovation and intrapreneurship. Given the required characteristics earlier, these are the components of IT infrastructure that enable rapid experiments.

Cloud Computing

Conventionally with on-premise technology, the size of the infrastructure footprint is limited by rigid budgeting cycles. Decisions about infrastructure have to be made upfront, and short-term change does not come easily between cycles.[20] I have experienced the process in various corporations. The cycle timings vary in different corporations but the overall process looks quite similar. It is an annual process that is triggered in a particular month every year. If the business year starts in January, the budgeting cycle would start around June the year before. All the leaders provide inputs for the budget, raising their requests for the upcoming year.

It takes around two months for departments to discuss their requirements, put in the numbers, debate the requests, and finally come to a submission. After the requests are gathered, it takes another two to three months for the corporate senior leaders and finance to come together to review the request, balancing the needs of different lines and functions. It is nearly year-end when the final decision is made. Once the budget is confirmed, the teams can engage procurement to source the required infrastructure. Procurement usually takes four to six months to onboard a vendor. The vendor will take another couple of months or even longer, depending on the scope of work, to complete the deployment. It is easily an 18-month lag from the initiation of the request until you actually get to use it. Imagine how devastated you'd be if you were working on an innovation that required infrastructure to support the development.

To move fast, your corporation needs an agile and scalable infrastructure. In contrast to on-premise infrastructure, cloud infrastructure is located off-premise and cloud servers are accessed via the Internet. With cloud infrastructure, users do not have to manage physical servers or run software applications on their own machines.[21] Cloud is much more than storing and sharing files on the Internet. One of the cloud components, cloud computing, offers delivery of computing services including servers, storage, databases, networking, software, analytics, and intelligence.[22]

Cloud computing eliminates the upfront capital expense of acquiring physical infrastructure and offers scalability in real time. Post setup, most cloud computing is self-service and on-demand, making it easy for users to manage the capacity on their own. Many cloud computing providers also offer emerging technology services, such as machine learning and artificial intelligence, data lakes and analytics, and the Internet of Things (IoT).

Cloud service providers usually charge on a "Pay-as-you-go" model. It is a cost-effective model that allows the corporation to easily adapt to changing business needs without overcommitting budgets. The corporation can pay based on needs, instead of the forecast. This model also provides transparency of charges. By paying for services on an as-required basis, cost savings can be redirected to innovation.[23]

Sandbox Environment

In the science world, experiments are conducted in a laboratory. It is a confined area with safety measures in place. In case anything goes wrong during the experiment, it can be shut down quickly. Any hazard is contained in the laboratory and does not affect the world outside. In a corporation, people face the fear of risking well-established operations whenever there is change. To provide a safe space for employees to experiment, you need a similar setup to a laboratory for experimentation.

The environment is called a sandbox. The word sandbox comes from the shallow and wide container filled with soft sand in which children can play. It is an environment in which kids can have fun and you would not worry about their safety. In the IT context, a sandbox is a testing environment that enables intrapreneurs to run and execute experiments without risking the application, system or platform on which the experiments run. Any work that is done in the sandbox can be iterated, improved, and refined, without affecting the experience of real customers. A sandbox speeds up innovation as it allows development and testing to happen in parallel. Only after the experiment is completed and the product is ready, it is transferred to and deployed into the production environment.

The sandbox environment takes away the psychological barrier and pressure of risking the existing business. It also provides a compartmental environment in which intrapreneurs need not worry about the integration with all the other systems at the experimental stage or else they can test one integration at a time. The beauty of a sandbox is the creative freedom that it offers to users.[24] It creates the environment to walk the talk of embracing failures. Depending on the innovation use case, sandbox setup and usage varies. Here are some examples to consider when setting up a sandbox:

- *Mimic the production environment.* Specify the list of essential functions in the sandbox that are replicated from the system in the production environment, including interaction with other systems. Some application programming interface (API)-enabled corporations provide an API sandbox as the production environment largely uses APIs. API, a powerful innovation infrastructure, will be further discussed later.
- *Datasets.* A sandbox can offer a limited dataset for testing purposes. Data can be a subset of real customer data, dummy, or synthesized data. The corporation needs to define what data go into or are prohibited from the sandbox.

- *Network connectivity.* The sandbox is an isolated environment and therefore, it should be specified whether it is allowed to connect with any other network. If the connectivity is allowed, a vulnerability assessment should be done to ensure that the connectivity is secure.
- *Access control.* Define who can have access to the sandbox, how the user applies for access, and how the access right is reviewed.
- *Life cycle of an experiment.* Specify how long the experiment will last, how long the assets of the experiment will be kept in the sandbox, the determining factors for shutting down an experiment, and how the data will be kept as a record.

Application Programming Interfaces

An API is a software intermediary that allows applications to talk to each other. It is a messenger that delivers your request to the provider and returns the provider's response to you. Figure 6.4 provides a simple explanation of APIs.

The API is not a new invention but its commercialization has gathered pace since the 2000s. It started when Salesforce chose the Internet as the host for its service and developed its approach using an API.[25] Subsequently, eBay launched its API in late 2000, together with a program for a select group of developers. In 2002, Amazon joined in when it launched Amazon Web Services. Fast forward to 2021 and the API has

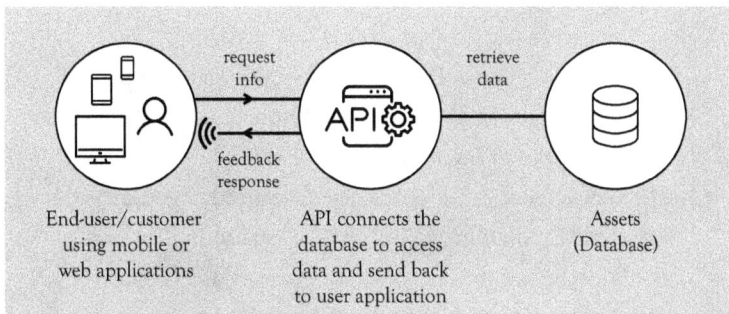

Figure 6.4 A simple explanation of APIs

become a powerful component gaining increasing traction in fields from e-commerce (Amazon and Shopify), consumer services (Uber, Spotify), social media (Instagram, Facebook, Twitter), and financial services (Visa, Mastercard, BBVA).

In its report "What It Really Takes to Capture the Value of APIs," McKinsey explains, "As the connective tissue linking ecosystems of technologies and organizations, APIs allow businesses to monetize data, forge profitable partnerships, and open new pathways for innovation and growth." In a later report published in 2020, it found that nearly a third (30.6 percent) of the 13,500 developers, testers, and executives it surveyed said that APIs played a role in their organizations' ability to respond to COVID-19.[26] Many utilized APIs for customer communications, powering remote work options, and quickly responding to regulatory changes and government initiatives. Of those working on digital transformation initiatives, 84.5 percent stated that APIs played a significant role in those initiatives.

APIs can be defined as open or private, depending on whether they target external or in-house developers. Open APIs, which are designed to give access to external third parties including customers, vendors, or partners, take innovation to the next level. Corporations can build new services by exposing their APIs to other businesses. In this book, however, the focus is on private APIs that are accessible by the employees of a corporation. The major objective of private APIs is to enable intrapreneurs to create new products for the corporation that leverage existing systems.

APIs have become the growth engine for innovation. By giving API access to your employees, you can facilitate intrapreneurship activities to:

- *Leverage existing assets.* Rather than creating siloed applications from scratch, private APIs enable intrapreneurs to draw from a common pool of internal software assets.[27]
- *Agile development.* APIs hasten the development and deployment cycle by enabling agility and automation. They also extend scalability, functionality, and ease of use.[28] They also save the time and effort needed to integrate internal IT systems.

- *Foster collaboration*. APIs make collaboration much easier.[29] Often people from one department will ask for information from another to facilitate their work. Opening the dataset, defining the access rights, and monitoring data usage is not easy. Sometimes people are put off asking because of the tremendous amount of work involved. With private APIs, many of these things can be done without hassle and the collaboration can flow more seamlessly.

A Practical Case Study of API Sandbox

As an intrapreneur, I often work on new ideas that require collaboration with external partners including startups and Financal Technology companies (FinTechs). In my previous role at a global bank, collaborating with external parties has never been an easy task. Banking is a highly regulated industry. Any experiment with external parties faces the concerns of compromising information security, mishandling customer data, and putting internal systems at risk. If those incidences happen, the consequence is huge including regulatory actions, fines, and loss of reputation. To avoid the potential risks, the bank has built a complicated due diligence and onboarding process for gatekeeping. The process usually takes more than six months to assess the external parties to ensure all their operating process and policies are compliant as required by the bank. It is a well-designed process to safeguard the bank's and its customers' interests.

However, imagine if I am at an early stage of discussion with a few FinTechs. All I want to do is to test whether they can perform the functions as they have claimed. To achieve that, I need to conduct a proof of concept with FinTech. I do not have the resources to onboard all of them and then start to test and select only one. Considering the process would take more than six months, by the time I can start testing them, the market opportunity might have gone.

To solve that, I have brought in the idea of using an external API sandbox. In this case, the API sandbox acts as the middle layer between the bank and the external parties. When I want to collaborate with a FinTech, the FinTech would register on the API sandbox. The complete registration takes around two days. Once the registration is done, FinTech can upload its

API documentation and also expose its API endpoints on the API sandbox. Since this sandbox is separate from the bank's production environment, no onboarding to the bank is required. My team only need to connect with the FinTech APIs using our corporate developer environment. Once that is done, we can proceed to call their APIs and test their functions. The setup of the testing environment is within days. Using this API sandbox, the team that I led can complete a proof of concept within one to two weeks.

Under this arrangement, there are still restrictions that the team need to observe. Since this is an external environment, only anonymized or synthetic data can be used. Once the proof of concept is over, the connection needs to be unplugged. If my team proceed with a pilot with FinTech, which would involve the production environment, we still need to complete the due diligence to safeguard the bank and its customers.

This setup expedites the testing and selection of FinTechs. There are no resources wasted to perform unnecessary due diligence on unqualified FinTechs. The team can also enter into the contracting stage with clear visibility of FinTech's capability.

Democratized Data

Data are an important asset that drives innovation. With access to data, intrapreneurs can discover trends, understand customers' needs, and explore potential solutions. Corporations are applying data and data analytics to drive decision making on innovation projects.[30] Netflix is a great example. By collecting data from its 151 million subscribers and implementing data analytics models, Netflix discovers customer behavior and buying patterns. It can even predict whether a show will be a hit when it is produced. By carefully analyzing datasets, Netflix noticed a correlation between fans of the original British House of Cards TV show and fans of both actor Kevin Spacey and director David Fincher.[31] So Netflix brought these three elements together in one drama, *House of Cards*. It instantly became its key show. In 2013, 86 percent of Netflix subscribers said they were less likely to cancel their subscription because of this one show alone.

Data are the new gold for corporate innovation. Thanks to technological advances, data are more readily available in today's business environment. But while many corporations have realized the power of data and relevant insights, many still fall short of providing data empowerment to employees. A MicroStrategy survey found that 46 percent of business intelligence (BI) and analytics respondents had been able to identify and create new products and revenue streams, and 45 percent of organizations were using data and analytics to develop new business models.[32] But only 32 percent of respondents said their organizations made data available to up to half of their employees. Worse, about a fifth (19 percent) gave no more than a quarter of their employees access to corporate data, and only 14 percent gave it to 75 percent of staff.

What's to be gained by giving all employees access to data? In a 2019 article for Raconteur, "Empowering Employees to Think Like Data Scientists," Ben Rossi quoted Elif Tutuk, senior director of research at Qlik.[33] Tutuk said, "By empowering all employees and nurturing data literacy, businesses may gain more than they could ever realize by looking beyond one sole data employee to make a good decision." The same applies to intrapreneurship. Data should no longer only be accessible and used by data scientists and data analytics teams. Employees from any part of the organization should be provided with access to data and intuitive self-service analytics tools. It allows them to apply data science to their respective business challenges and explore innovation based on their understanding of the challenges.

To democratize data in your corporation, you need the following infrastructure components:

- *Data marketplace.* A hub where data are hosted for employees to access. Ideally, it should be self-service and users can define the rules of data that they require (e.g., data element within which period, parameters, and filters).
- *Self-service analytics.* Easy-to-use data analytics tools for nontechnical users. Functions can include drag-and-drop discovery, natural language processing inquiry, visualization, and so on.
- *No-code AI/ML.* AI models that require no coding skill to build. These models are often visual. This reduces the entry barrier and time to build AI models and enables non-AI-trained employees to easily experiment with the technology.

- *Data literacy training.* Even though the technical barrier has been lowered with the aforementioned infrastructure, you still need to provide training for employees to understand the data, the basic skills required, and also troubleshooting.

Questions for corporate leaders:

- What IT infrastructure do you have in your organization to support intrapreneurship?
- Do you have a roadmap to acquire the components of the previously mentioned IT infrastructure?

While you are making the effort to build the necessary structures for idea management and portfolio management, as well as IT infrastructure, you also need to consider how to safeguard the value of these ideas. They could be of great potential value to your business so taking early steps to protect intellectual property (IP) can enhance the competitiveness of your business. In the next section, we will discuss managing the IP from intrapreneurship activities.

Intellectual Property Management

Managing IP for new product development is a critical factor in the successful commercialization of a product. There are four major categories of IP: patents, copyright laws, trademarks, and trade secrets. Based on different stages of innovation, the IP consideration will vary. Intrapreneurs are seldom IP experts. Based on the stage of work that the intrapreneurs have embarked on, corporations should provide support and resources for them to access advice and guidance on navigating the IP process. While I cannot provide legal advice on IP, I will try my best to offer an overall picture of what IP management looks like in the context of corporate innovation. Your corporation should make relevant decisions based on the advice of your own IP legal counsel.

What follows are the IP factors to consider along the innovation journey.

Early-Stage Discovery and Ideation Phase

During this stage, the main activities involved are research and discovery. Two considerations come into play.

First, third-party registered IPs. Does the idea involve using any asset with IP that has been registered by others? Does any part of the proposed product rely on patented technology or a design that is owned by another company? If so, the corporation needs to consider this when the product is developed. The corporation should assist in assessing whether the IP is available for licensing and the cost associated with it. It will affect the decision on proceeding with and commercializing the idea.

Second, the corporation can consider protecting the information as trade secrets.[34] At this early stage, there is limited claim toward registering any IP, since the idea has not been fully developed. In fact, not all commercially viable ideas can be registered due to the fulfillment criteria associated with different IPs. At this stage, the corporation can try to manage the idea as trade secrets to avoid alerting competitors. For information to qualify as trade secrets, it has to be[35] (the definition might vary across jurisdictions):

- *Commercially valuable* because it is secret;
- Known only to a *limited group of persons*; and
- Be subject to *reasonable steps taken* by the rightful holder of the information to keep it secret, including the use of confidentiality agreements for business partners and employees.

Any unauthorized acquisition, use, or disclosure of information by others, in a manner contrary to honest commercial practices, would be considered an unfair practice and a violation of trade secret protection. However, the level of protection is limited under trade secrets. You cannot stop another company from developing a similar idea or disclosing a similar idea that it has developed independently.

Development Phase

When intrapreneurs enter this phase of development, it's likely that the product concept has already been formed and the team will start building the product. In this phase, intrapreneurs need to consider the potential IPs of the product. Examples under different IP categories during this stage, on top of trade secrets, can be:

- Patent: concept, invention, design, technology know-how, functionality, process
- Copyright: Source code written, elements in the user interface

Do bear in mind that patent and copyright are two distinct concepts and each is designed to protect different aspects of the product. Copyright protects the expression of the idea but not the idea itself, while a patent protects the idea. So if you have developed a software, a copyright is designed to protect the code written while a patent protects its unique functionalities. Hence, you need to consider thoroughly what makes the most sense for the protection your product requires. You will also need to consider a commercialization plan. If you plan to sell the licensing of the product to a third party, the patent would clarify your ownership of the product. Putting the right protection in place would help set up your success in commercializing a product.

Commercialization Phase

Assuming that your product is now ready to be launched onto the market and you already have the necessary patent and copyright protection, there is one more IP you should consider before launch: trademark. A product needs strong branding, and trademarks are information signals that innovative companies can use to distinguish the quality of new products and services.[36] On the other hand, a trademark is also an alternative option for differentiating your new product if it is not eligible for patent registration.

When it comes to employee IP ownership, many corporations are reluctant to consider this as an option. The reason is that managing an employee-owned IP could be complicated, especially when the corporation relies on the IP to run a business. Handled inappropriately, there could be potential tension and even litigation. But let's set aside the implications for the corporation for a moment. Does the intrapreneur who creates a new product have grounds to claim the IP from a legal perspective? This might vary based on jurisdiction.

Let's look at some examples:

- U.S. Chamber of Commerce: In the United States, when a worker employed by a company is directly involved in the process and creation of a new, patentable idea for the business, the employer owns any IP created by that employee.[37] This is viewed as the employee simply doing their job. But what if an employee's direct role is one where they don't work directly on a product or system that will eventually be patented by the business? In this scenario, the employee technically owns the innovation, and the business is afforded a nonexclusive license to use that innovation without paying any royalties to the employee. The employee, however, can license their idea to other businesses independent of the employer. This is the case even if the employee used an employer's resources to create the product or service improvement.

- Australian government: In Australia, the employer owns the IP created by an employee if it is related to the employer's business unless the employment contract stipulates otherwise.[38] Under common law, the issue is whether the invention was made in the course of the employee's employment and whether it was the employee's role to invent, that is, whether they had a "duty to invent." This is frequently dealt with in the terms of the contract of employment, although the contract may not always be determinative in deciding whether or not the employee owns the patent.

- Singapore: If the IP is created in the course of employment or under the terms of employment, the employer is the owner unless otherwise agreed.[39] An invention or design made by an employee belongs to the employer if it is made in the course of the normal duties of, or specifically assigned to, the employee. There is no statutory requirement to compensate employees for trademarks. For patents and designs, there is no requirement for the employee to be equitably rewarded for the creation of the IP.

Ultimately, it depends on the jurisdiction and circumstances when it comes to employee ownership of IP. Many corporations think they have the total right to claim all IP during the course of employment. And some employment contracts also contain special clauses that give employers rights over employees' ideas or inventions, even if they have nothing to do with their jobs.

> Question for corporate leaders:
>
> Does your organization provide support to intrapreneurs to manage an intellectual property?

Intrapreneurship Metrics

You can't manage what you don't measure.

—Peter Drucker

Having the right metrics helps ensure you are heading in the right direction. Just as corporate leaders use metrics to measure key aspects of a business, they need to apply the same to intrapreneurship. Having a set of metrics gives you a better picture of intrapreneurship activities and guides your employees on which important intrapreneurship activities to measure.

A few basic metrics to start with:

1. The number of ideas generated by employees
2. The number of intrapreneurship projects
3. The number of MVPs launched by intrapreneurs
4. Customer satisfactory level of the MVP launched

These are common ones to start with for corporations to start keeping track of intrapreneurship activities. These metrics encourage the robustness of intrapreneurship.

Depending on the maturity of intrapreneurship in your organization, you can plan to introduce different metrics at different stages. Corporations that are more mature in intrapreneurship would like to measure their investment efficiency.

More advanced metrics could include:

1. Revenue/profit generated by the new intrapreneur-led products, for example, 3M's 30 percent rule: 30 percent of each division's revenues must come from products introduced in the last four years.[40]
2. ROI of the new intrapreneur-led products.

These metrics provide more quantified results of the corporation's investment in intrapreneurship. However, introducing advanced metrics too early can be intimidating to employees. These metrics might put people off coming up with new ideas as they are worried about the revenue or ROI requirements. Revenue can also be a tricky indicator as a new product usually takes time to ramp up sales. Measuring the revenue on a single-year basis with a newly launched product could be misleading. Refer to "Asking for immediate ROI" in Chapter 11 to see how asking for ROI too early can put innovation at risk.

A well-planned system measuring the right metrics can help you analyze what went wrong in the process if the outcomes are not as expected. What if, over time, the revenue from the new intrapreneur-led product is low? Using the metrics, leaders can now identify the problem: do they not have a sufficient number of new MVPs by intrapreneurs? Or do they have many MVPs but not all generate good revenue? Do they have a sufficient number of ideas to start with? And did a good portion get funded? With the metrics above, you can troubleshoot specific areas.

It's best to keep metrics simple and easy to understand. Having too many and too complicated metrics can confuse employees. It usually makes the metrics hard to follow and they soon become obsolete.

Question for corporate leaders:

How do you measure intrapreneurship in your organization?

In this chapter, we've looked at the various components of corporate infrastructure that your employees can leverage. These processes, procedures, protocols, policies, and systems enable employees to progress their ideas. In addition, your corporate strategy plays a significant role in your innovation strategy. It greatly influences how you prioritize ideas to invest in and the capabilities you need to acquire to progress those ideas.

To visualize all the ideas in the corporation, you need to build a platform for idea management and manage the pipeline. You need to monitor all the ideas in the portfolio to understand their potential impact on your business. Finally, you need to invest in the relevant IT infrastructure and provide IP advice and support to protect the IPs created from new ideas. You also need to start measuring intrapreneurship to identify any gap between your input and output, and how you can improve it.

In the next chapter, we will dive deep into how to prepare the most important asset of intrapreneurship—your people. Most of your employees probably never imagined creating a business themselves. They were told they had a specific job for which they were hired, and yet now you are encouraging them to innovate. How can you help them get outside of their comfort zones? In the next chapter, we will discuss the skills and training that your people need to develop their ideas.

CHAPTER 7

Essential Skills of Intrapreneurs

You have your culture and infrastructure ready. You might even have received a couple of good ideas from your employees. You and your leadership team have excitedly sponsored some of them, hoping they would drive future businesses. But three months have gone by, and nothing much has happened. Then six months in, your employees tell you they're still at the initial stage, just clarifying the details. A year later, nothing has been launched. You are, quite rightly, wondering what went wrong. And the answer is usually quite simple: your employees may be passionate but they're not equipped to be intrapreneurs just yet.

If you are looking to groom intrapreneurial talents, use this chapter as a guide to developing your people. Learn the basic concepts of the required skills and understand how they will help your organization innovate. Evaluate your list of potential intrapreneurs, which you identified in Chapter 3, against the list of skills in this chapter. See where the gaps are and explore how you can help your intrapreneurs acquire those skills. You can also use this chapter to review whether or not you have the skills to innovate for your organization. See which skills are new to you and how you can upskill to lead the organization by example.

The breadth and depth of skills required by employees vary over time. Traditionally in large corporations, employees specialize in one domain and work on a set of predefined tasks throughout their careers. The early twentieth-century work system was designed to maximize productivity. It made employees experts in a particular area and little beyond that. This group of employees is called the "I-shaped talents," with the vertical part of the letter "I" representing their depth of domain expertise. In an article published in *Harvard Business Review* in 2001, Hansen and Oetinger introduced the T-shaped manager.[1] This is a new kind of executive who breaks out of the traditional corporate hierarchy to share knowledge freely across the organization (the horizontal part of the T) while remaining fiercely committed to individual business unit performance (the vertical part).

In 2013, Tom Wessel, author at SolutionsIQ, suggested that as the team matures, the next evolution is Pi-shaped. According to Wessel, Pi-shaped makes an excellent metaphor for truly adaptive team members. Rather than one area of expertise, a Pi-shaped team member possesses two. But now, with rapid technological advancement and the changing market landscape in the era of Industry 5.0, it is time to move on from Pi-shaped talent. Dr. Esin Akay refers to comb-shaped talents— employees whose skills are broad but with multiple areas of expertise in the shape of a comb.[2] These multiple expertise areas might never be deep enough as the knowledge of a truly deep specialist is only in one area. However, this is not a disadvantage considering the interconnected and interdependent world that we live in. Comb-shaped talents are agile, life-long learners and they collaborate with others by having sufficient depth in several domains. Figure 7.1 illustrates how the I-, T-, Pi-, and comb-shaped talents are different in terms of breath and depth of knowledge.

To become intrapreneurs, employees need to develop themselves as comb-shaped talents. In terms of depth, they need to adapt and swiftly learn domain expertise based on the ideas that they are working on. In terms of breadth, they should develop broad business knowledge to enhance how they lead the team to commercialize the idea. Comb-shaped talents truly differentiate themselves by their ability to learn fast and adapt to various settings.

Being intrapreneurial starts with one's mindset but mindset alone is not sufficient for coming up with a great idea and making that idea a

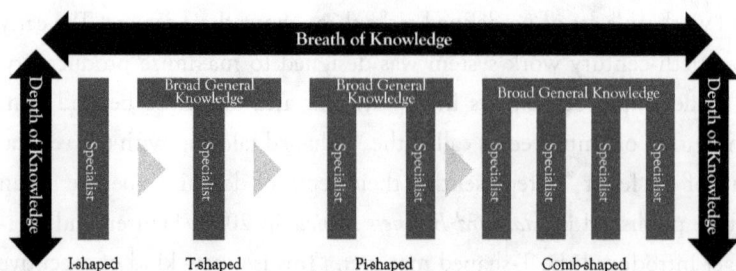

Figure 7.1 *I-, T-, Pi-, and comb-shaped talents*

reality in a large organization. In the rest of this chapter, we will talk about the various skills an intrapreneur needs to master. Depending on the domain areas that you are innovating in, the subject matter will differ. For example, if you are working for a logistics company and looking into ideas for automated goods tracking, an intrapreneur might need IoT device knowledge. Those in the banking industry exploring instant, cross-border payments might need to study blockchain technology. What you need to learn in the form of vertical expertise depends on your field, the current applications, and the relevant technology trends.

That said, there are fundamental skills that every intrapreneur should develop, which apply across industries and domains. There are four broad categories of essential skills:

1. *Disciplined innovation process.* A set of skills and methodologies that you need to acquire and learn to identify problems, come up with ideas, and validate and convert ideas into a profitable business. It also includes skills that help you build a bridge between an idea and the actual launch. It helps you organize the project in a structured manner so you and your team have a clear path of execution.
2. *Leadership.* Skills that you need to inspire, lead without authority, motivate, and collaborate with other people inside and outside of your corporation.
3. *Navigating the organization.* Skills that you need to navigate a large organization and convince the stakeholders to move your idea forward.
4. *Communications.* Skills that you need to effectively communicate your ideas with other people.

Figure 7.2 summarizes the essential skills that an intrapreneur needs to master.

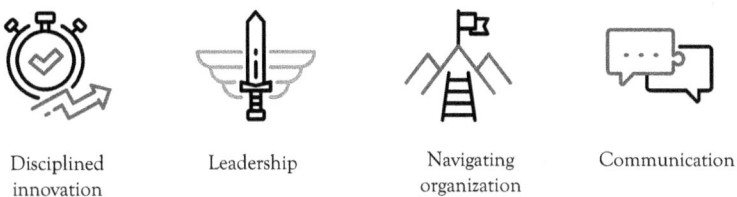

| Disciplined innovation | Leadership | Navigating organization | Communication |

Figure 7.2 Four skills that intrapreneurs need to master

Questions for corporate leaders:

- Which talent shape (I-, T-, Pi-, comb-) do the majority of your employees belong to?
- Do your employees possess the skills of intrapreneurs?

In the rest of this chapter, I present the methodologies and tools published by innovation pioneers, my own experience of using them, and how others have used them. An experienced intrapreneur should choose the tools based on the situation, adjust the framework to fit the purpose, and understand what works for the people in their corporation. For further reading about each of these skills, consult the recommended resources in each section.

Disciplined Innovation Process

While creativity requires freedom to grow, innovation requires discipline. Amateurs come up with ideas occasionally, like accidental thoughts. But innovation practitioners who generate numerous ideas rely on disciplined innovation methodologies to spark continuous inspiration. Learn the following innovation methodologies to understand how to generate unlimited ideas, evaluate whether those ideas are good enough, and break down big ideas into new launches.

First, let's look at the cycles involved in delivering an innovative product. Three innovation methodologies guide you through the cycle, from understanding the problem to launching and scaling a product. The innovation methodologies are:

1. Problem-solving using design thinking
2. Launching minimum viable product (MVP) using lean startup
3. Scaling the product using agile

Each methodology addresses different objectives using different tools and techniques. There are also overlapping areas of these methodologies. Combining these innovation methodologies provides a structured

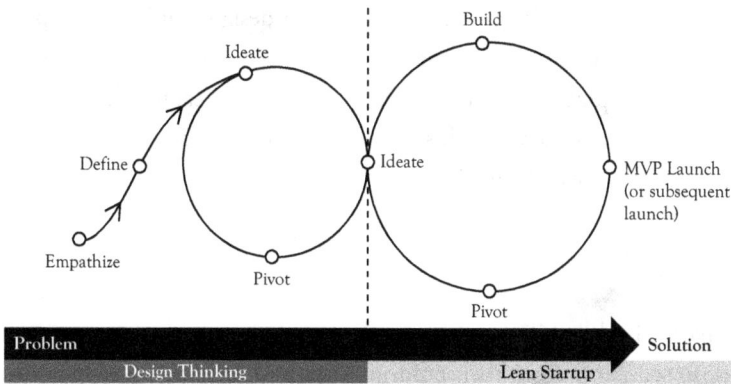

Figure 7.3 Cycle of innovation combining design thinking and lean startup

framework for you to execute your ideas. Figure 7.3 is a diagram that shows how a combination of design thinking, lean startup, and agile can work together. This figure helps visualize what the cycle of innovation looks like when design thinking and lean startup methodology are combined.

The execution of innovation projects is often not linear, with one stage ending and another phase starting without overlapping. So corporations should not segregate the phases to be carried out by entirely different teams and design collaboration only at the touchpoints of different phases. The use of different methodologies and activities should be viewed as a continuous and iterative process.

Problem Solving by Design Thinking

Most people know design from graphic design or packaging design, which relates to the appearance of a product. It's not surprising as these are visual and relatable; we can see and touch the design. Design thinking is something different. It is a process of customer-centric creative problem solving.

People who've gone through education and become industrial designers, user experience designers, or user interface designers often practice design thinking. But you do not necessarily need to be trained as a designer. It doesn't matter whether or not you can sketch, use design software, or speak design language because design thinking is a problem-solving skill. I'll discuss the approach and the process but it's just as important to practice it hands-on by applying it to real problems.

The best way to avoid this problem is with the following four-step process: empathize, define, ideate, and validate.

Empathize

Empathy is the ability to emotionally understand what other people feel, to see things from their point of view, and imagine yourself in their place. It is you putting yourself in someone else's position and feeling what they must be feeling.[3] It's a powerful ability that allows you to connect with different people, even though you might not come from the same background or have not experienced exactly what they have been through. Empathize guides problem solving by first understanding the customer. According to "The Field Guide to Human-Centered Design" by IDEO,[4] empathy is a "deep understanding of the problems and realities of the people you are designing for."

Empathize is an important stage that facilitates subsequent ideation of good product design. Emi Kolawole, editor-in-residence of Stanford University d.school, said, "I can't come up with any new ideas if all I do is exist in my own life."[5]

Questions for intrapreneurs:

- What is your personal experience of empathy toward others?
- When was the last time you applied empathy to your customers?

Depending on the problem you are trying to solve, the first step is to visualize your customers' attitudes and behaviors, bringing them to life on an empathy map. An empathy map allows you and your team to articulate and form a common ground of understanding with customers to discover their needs. Figure 7.4 is a template of an empathy map.

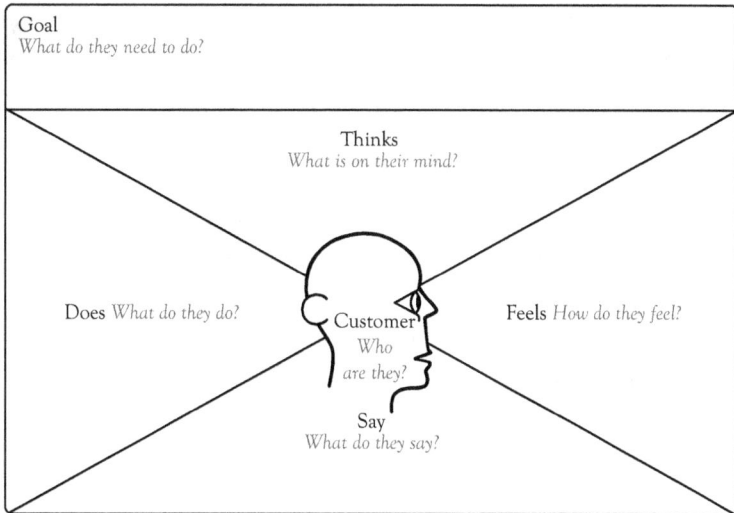

Figure 7.4 Empathy map

Here's a step-by-step guide to completing the empathy map:

1. *Customer.* Profile your customer by giving them a name, age, job, and lifestyle. Build a comprehensive profile by giving more details. The best approach is to profile a real customer that you have dealt with.
2. *Goal.* What is your customer's goal? Think of the bigger picture beyond the immediate problem that you are solving. Is the customer thinking about their next promotion, achieving financial freedom, work–life balance, or retirement? This helps you visualize how solving the problem aligns with their prioritized goals.
3. *Says.* Quote what the customer says during their daily life or your interaction with them. What words does the customer use to describe their problem?
4. *Thinks.* Capture what the customer is thinking. What is on their mind? What matters to them? What are they thinking but are reluctant to say? Discover why they are hesitant to unveil their real thoughts.
5. *Does.* What action does the customer take? How did they try to solve it in the past? What alternatives have they tried?
6. *Feels.* What is the emotional status of the customer? How do they feel about this problem? Are they worried, concerned, excited, or annoyed?

An empathy map is something you can kickstart anytime since it is an early-stage exercise. There are various sources of information that you can bring into it. The team can collectively profile customers by:

- *Past customer interaction.* If you have direct interaction with customers, you can refer to your experience with them. Quote what they have told you or what you have observed in the past about the issue.
- *Sales input.* If you do not have direct access to customers, go to a salesperson who owns the customer relationship and seek their help to provide insights. Tell the salesperson that you are working on solving a problem for the customer and will require their help to crystalize the need. Try not to lead the conversation into a discussion of solutions as this is too early.
- *Customer service data.* Data can be a good tool as they present an unbiased view of what the problem is. You can see how the customer deals with the problem. How many calls or complaints did your company get that are relevant to the problem? What did the customer say when they made the call? Were they emotional about the issue?
- *Interview a customer.* This is a good source but it needs to be managed with care. It depends on the relationship you have with the customer. If the customer is very open and welcoming, by all means, do it. But if you are not directly handling the relationship or the customer does not have a particularly warm relationship with you, start with your internal resources instead of talking to them. At this stage, since you do not have much to offer in terms of problem definition or solution, the customer could be confused about why you need a conversation.

When you do talk to customers to understand how they view the problem, it is important to differentiate what they say they want versus what they actually need. For that reason, the technique of asking the "5 Whys" can be helpful. The "5 Whys" was originally developed by Sakichi Toyoda and was used within the Toyota Motor Corporation during the evolution of its manufacturing methodologies. It was a critical component of problem-solving training, delivered as part of the induction into the Toyota Production System. Taiichi Ohno, the architect of the Toyota Production System, said that the basis of the approach was to ask "why?" five times whenever we find a problem. By repeating "why?" five times, the nature of the problem, as well as its solution, becomes clear.[6] In the context of design thinking, the "5 Whys" are applied similarly but the Whys are asked in such a way as to discover the root desire of the customer.

You should focus on the customer first and not the idea. In fact, this is a common mistake. People are obsessed with ideas that will change the world, and immediately they start thinking about how to make them happen. But once they jump ahead to focus on the solution, they never go back to understand the actual problem or what the customer really wants. Skipping the empathize phase can quickly lead to failure if the final solution can't help the customer. Or you might end up with a quick fix, catering to a superficial problem but not the customer's real need. This could make the product weak and you would lose the opportunity to address the problem with a game-changer.

Define

With the insights gathered from the empathize phase, you have sufficient information to proceed to the define phase. Define is a phase in which you synthesize all the information you gathered in the empathize phase. The target outcome is to have a clearly defined and actionable problem statement.

A problem statement defines the unmet need of a customer. The insights you synthesized from the empathy map, and also the "5 Whys," should be considered when you frame the problem statement. Later on, when you brainstorm solutions in the ideation stage, the solutions should always point to solving the problem you have defined. A clearly defined problem statement keeps the team focused and provides a clear goal and objective.

The format of a problem statement is as follows:

As (the customer), when I (in a scenario/conducting the job to be done), I would like to have (ideal experience), so that I can (achieve my primary goal).

When you form the problem statement, you need to examine it and see whether it fits the following criteria to make it a good problem statement for the subsequent innovation phase.

1. *Does it identify the customer?* Is there any description of the customer that you are targeting? Are they young graduates? Are they owners of small businesses? Are they working couples with children? Make sure you describe the customer who is experiencing the problem.

2. *Does it focus on the need of the customer?* The customer's perspective always comes first under the design thinking methodology. The problem statement should focus on describing the customer's goal and need, instead of those of your corporation. Try to avoid having your corporation's perspective in it. For example, a good problem statement should contain wording like "Working couples with children (customers) need a convenient way to prepare for meals so that they can spend more quality time together" instead of "Our company needs to design a convenient way of preparing meals for working couples with children so that we can capture market share and make more profit."

3. *Is it sufficiently broad?* Is the scope of the problem broad enough to explore solutions? There is usually more than one way you can solve a problem. The problem statement should not point to one, and only one, solution. It should also not contain a description of the solution itself. However, the problem should not be so broad it has no focus. It is impossible to solve all of the world's issues using a single problem statement. Try not to include too many problems of different causes.

It's important to validate the problem statement and pain point. Validation is an important gatekeeping exercise in the design thinking process. Before you proceed to explore the solution, you need to validate whether the problem you have identified is something the customer really wants to be solved. The problem statement you have crafted and the visual presentation of how it works currently is good artifact to start with. Create a simple discussion guide to facilitate the conversation with your customer, building on the information you already have. A simple discussion guide can include questions like:

1. From our research, we have identified the [problem statement]. How do you relate to this statement?
2. Can you walk us through the process the last time you performed this task? How did you feel?
3. From the study, we believe there are some pain points involved. [Visualize the pain points in the as-is scenario.] Which pain point do you relate to?
4. Is there any other pain point that we have missed? Can you describe it?
5. Which pain point(s) is/are the most pressing?
6. How would solving these pain points make you feel?

From the discussion with an engaged customer, you should have sufficient information to validate the problem statement. The bottom line is that your subsequent work should be based on a problem that the customer recognizes as an actual problem, one with enough pain that they want it to be solved now, if not yesterday.

Questions for intrapreneurs:

- From your past experience, do you frame and validate your problem statement before moving on to working on the solution?
- How do you think the technique might help in your upcoming projects?

Ideate

After you have framed and validated the problem statement, it is time to move on to the ideation phase. You will now brainstorm solutions that can solve the problem that's been defined. Ideation is probably the most exciting part of the design thinking process. It is the stage to set your mind free and explore as many ideas as possible before you land on any. Ideation works better as a group exercise so I would strongly suggest that you form your team (refer to Chapter 8, "Diversity as Multipliers") or seek relevant stakeholders or allies to brainstorm together. The more ideas you can gather during this stage, the better the results could be. The quantity of ideas matters at the early stage of ideation as you want to capture diverse thinking.

To shift the mindset of the team from focusing on problems, you can make the transition by forming a "How might we…?" statement. A "How might we…" statement looks something like this: "How might we design a solution that can [achieve the goal of the customer described under the problem statement]?"

If I had asked the public what they wanted, they would have said a faster horse.
> —Henry Ford, founder of Ford Motor Company

Some people mistake design thinking as hearing what the customer says and providing them with what they asked for. It is, in fact, much deeper than that. The best solution might not be what the client has explicitly asked for or could have imagined. The perfect solution most likely has not yet appeared on the market, since you are still trying to solve the problem. Do not limit yourself only to solutions that you have heard from customers or what other companies are doing. Encourage weird or wild ideas during brainstorming. Do not criticize any idea at this stage. But at the same time, you need to stay away from groupthink at the beginning of the ideation phase. Based on my experience, a good way to arrange ideation without groupthink is as follows:

1. Form a diverse brainstorming group. Gather people of diverse backgrounds and domains in a room for ideation. Try to not have more than half of the people from the same domain. Get everyone in sync on the problem the team is brainstorming. Given them sufficient background in the way of insights drawn from the empathize phase.

Provide everyone with the problem statement and the "How might we?" statement.

2. *Start with individual brainstorming in silence.* Set a time-bound individual exercise during which each person needs to come up with at least five ideas on their own. There should not be any upper limit on the number of ideas. Everyone has to work silently and no conversation among group members is allowed at this stage.

3. *Share.* Each member takes turns and shares their five ideas. The objective is to allow other members to understand the high-level concept of the solution, not the details. Set a time limit for each team member, for example, five minutes. Ensure everyone has a chance to go through all their ideas. Be open to listening to others' ideas and try not to interrupt any sharing, debate whether the idea works, or attempt to change anyone's idea.

4. *Synthesize.* On a whiteboard, group all similar or relevant ideas together until you have different clusters of ideas. Name each cluster using a broad solution name. Now the group should have several concepts for broad solutions.

Now that you have those broad-solution concepts, you need to prioritize the solutions to be explored, since you cannot act on all ideas at once with finite resources. When considering which idea to prioritize, you can use the idea prioritization matrix. In the matrix, one axis should be the impact on customers and the other should be the impact on your corporation. Finding the right solution to solve the customer problem is the main objective, but it would be meaningless if it does not benefit your corporation at all. Once you have the matrix up, allow the group to discuss what they think of each idea. Place the idea concepts onto the matrix to visualize where they sit. Figure 7.5 shows a two-by-two matrix that guides leaders and intrapreneurs to prioritize the ideas.

Validate the Idea

Once you have prioritized an idea, you should proceed to validate it. The idea is still very much a concept at this stage and there is no guarantee that it will work. Certainly, there is no way your corporation would

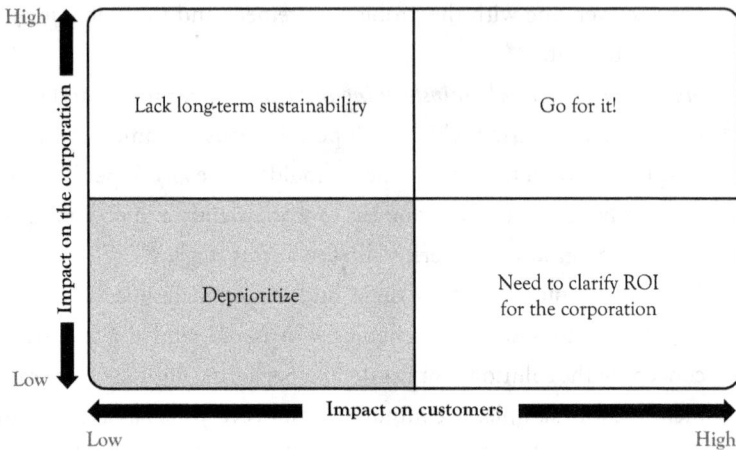

High ↑

Impact on the corporation

| Lack long-term sustainability | Go for it! |
| Deprioritize | Need to clarify ROI for the corporation |

Low ↓

◀━ Impact on customers ━▶

Low   High

Figure 7.5 Idea prioritization matrix

write a half-million-dollar check to invest in an idea based on a high-level concept. To build credibility, you need to validate it from different perspectives by considering three aspects: desirability, feasibility, and viability. A good idea should fulfill all three aspects. Passing it through the lens of validation, you should be able to tell whether a product is wanted by the customer, whether it can be built, and whether it makes commercial sense.

Desirability, feasibility, and viability are common validations required for any entrepreneur who is launching a new business. However, intrapreneurship demands more. Since intrapreneurs are innovating within a corporate context, corporate strategy and proprietary assets also need to be considered. Let's go into all of these in more detail. Figure 7.6 shows the sweet spot of a good intrapreneurship idea.

Desirability: Is your idea what your customers desire?

During the empathize phase, you validated the problem. Now you should validate whether the solution you propose is what the customer wants. Usually from the customer's perspective, it is a question of whether your solution solves the right pain points. A good validation approach is to build a low-fidelity prototype from your idea to share with customers and ask for their feedback. The beauty of a low-fidelity prototype is that it is cheap and fast to make and it can take any form as long as it helps to illustrate your idea. It could be a flow chat, concept presentation, mockup

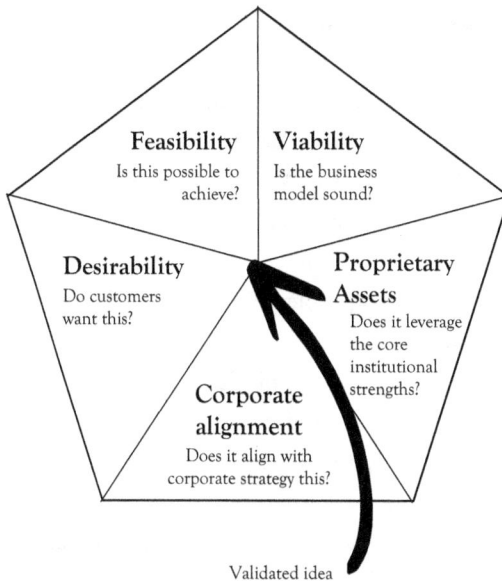

Figure 7.6 Validating an intrapreneurship idea

model, wireframes, or some sketched-out screenshots. Plan a discussion guide with a list of questions you want to validate with the customer. Stay open and do not force the solution onto them. Let them tell you what they think works or does not work. Ask the customer whether they consider your solution to be a painkiller that addresses their biggest pain or just a vitamin that eases the issue.

Feasibility: Is your idea concept possible to achieve?

You can have the most perfect idea and yet it is meaningless if the idea cannot be achieved in the real world. A time machine is a good example! People want it so badly that it keeps appearing in movies and fiction. It is a perfect solution for any regret you have in life. But technology-wise, it just cannot be built. Humanity cannot yet bring the solution to life. So a good idea needs to be possible and work as promised. Are the capability and technology that the idea relies on mature enough, and do they even exist? To test whether the idea can be developed, conduct a proof of concept. Break down the important components of the idea, for example, front end, back end, logic, platform, and interface, and design experiments to test risky assumptions around those components.

Viability: Can you build a viable business model from the idea?

After you have validated that customers do want your idea and it is achievable, the next important question is whether you can make a commercial case. It does not matter how good your solution is if customers do not want to pay for it or if the price is not sufficient to cover the costs of building and maintaining it. Validating viability can be challenging when your solution does not exist today. But you can estimate what the solution is worth. One approach is to look into whether customers are already paying for this problem to be solved. If there are alternative solutions in the market today, check out their cost. See how they compare with your idea. Hopefully, your idea is better than the existing ones (and it should be) and you can use the price as a baseline and charge a premium. However, this baseline approach might not be for the best if your solution really offers a best-in-class experience. That is, it's a true painkiller compared to all existing solutions. Benchmarking with those for pricing might not reflect its true value. Plus, if you are working on a problem with limited existing solutions, the benchmark might not be accurate. In that case, you can find out what it really costs your customers today for not solving the problem. How much time and effort are they spending? How many people do they hire to handle the current problem? These are more accurate factors that enable you to quantify the price your customers are paying.

Corporate alignment: Does your idea align with your corporate strategy?

As an intrapreneur, you are innovating within a corporation. Eventually, you hope that your idea will become a new product, a new solution, or even a new business for your corporation. Therefore, you should seek alignment with the corporate strategy. That would include the problem that you are working on, the customers you are targeting, and the ideas that you explore. Imagine if you are working in a food and beverage company that operates a fast-food chain as its sole business. But you discover a problem in the pharmaceutical industry that you are passionate about working on. Clearly, the target customers are entirely different from the fast-food customers. Your idea is to launch a new pharmaceutical business. I am not saying it's absolutely impossible. But it would be rare for a food and beverage corporation to take such a big risk if it is not already in the strategic plan. So look at the strategic plan that your corporation has for the next three to five years and see where your idea might sit in that plan. It will help tremendously when you pitch the idea to management.

Proprietary assets: Does your idea leverage core institutional strengths?

Each corporation has its core strengths and proprietary assets, which are exhibited in its technological know-how, patents, operational model, branding, clientele, financials, partnerships, and so on. Does your idea build on the strengths and assets of your corporation? How much does it rely on existing strengths or does it require an entirely new build? It is more sensible to sponsor an idea that can be built using 80 percent of the existing corporate capability and build 20 percent new capability than the other way around. On the other hand, consider how your idea, when accomplished, brings new proprietary assets that complement existing assets. Ask yourself how your idea strengthens your corporation's competitive advantage.

Intrapreneurship in Action: IBM—Pivoting Into a Design-Led Intrapreneurial Enterprise

In 2012, IBM hired a new CEO, Ginni Rometty. On her second day in post, she told the employees that customer experience would be fundamental to the transformation of IBM.[7] Phil Gilbert, head of Design, and Karel Vredenburg, director of Design, were given a mission by Ginni to create a global sustainable culture of design and design thinking. Before joining IBM, Phil worked for Lombardi, a company IBM acquired in 2009. According to Karel, Lombardi did not have any technology that was new to IBM but it did have an awesome way of designing it. Phil also created a version of design thinking for large enterprises.

With the mission defined by Ginni, the question the team had was how could they make that happen in an organization with 380,000 employees? Karel and his team took on the challenge. Given the scale of IBM, the transformation was a multiyear mission. At the time, IBM had about 200 designers. In the space of five years, it hired designers

(Continues)

(*Continued*)

in the fields of visual design, user experience, industrial design, and design research. By 2017, it had about 1,600 designers and 44 design studios around the world. Phil and Karel scaled design thinking across product, service, sales, and human resources functions. They built a design-led culture by focusing on user outcomes and building diverse and empowered teams.

Design thinking changed the way people approach problems at IBM. Using design thinking, IBM teams are able to build solutions from the users' perspective and create truly differentiating value for those solutions. To make the transformation sustainable, a special program was created. Employees were provided with tools, best practices, and a community that enabled them to study for an IBM design thinking badge. The plan has been a great success. In 2013, just seven teams obtained design thinking badges. By 2017, over 100,000 employees and hundreds of teams achieved this accolade.

Launching MVP by Lean Startup

Now that you have an idea you believe can solve the problem, it's time to put it into development. Some product ideas are huge and challenging to pull off. If your idea is big, there could be a lot of components you need to take care of. It is wonderful to imagine that your idea solves everything but we all know that, in reality, it cannot. And for you to execute the idea, you would not be able to deliver all the features in one go. It is simply impossible given the limited time and resources. If you choose to launch only when all the features are ready, you'll end up delivering the product two years from now and the market demand will already have shifted.

The more sensible way is to think big and start small. You should plan to deliver a good-enough product in a quick turnaround time, hit the market, gather learnings, and revise your offering accordingly. To achieve that, you need to define your MVP, which includes a subset of all the features of your ultimate product. In his book *The Lean Startup*, Eric Ries defined the MVP as a "version of a new product which allows a team to collect the maximum amount of validated learning about customers with the least effort."[8] A good example of MVP is LinkedIn. LinkedIn was first launched in May 2003. At that time, it had only the basic features of user profiles and a search function to help people find other users and send e-mail requests. Looking at the interface, it was nothing fancy.

If you're not embarrassed by the first version of your product, you've launched too late.

—Reid Hoffman, cofounder of LinkedIn

The purpose of the MVP is to:

- Build a good-enough product.
- Test your hypothesis and assumptions.
- Gather learnings from the market.
- Use the learnings to pivot.
- Help plan the next launch.

Even though the MVP is a good-enough version, it should NOT be:

- An incomplete product that does not serve its purpose
- A semifinished product
- A broken experience

As you can see in Figure 7.7, an MVP should offer some elements of functionality, usability, reliability, and a delightful experience. If an MVP has none of those things, you need to go back to the drawing board. The figure illustrates what an MVP is and is not.

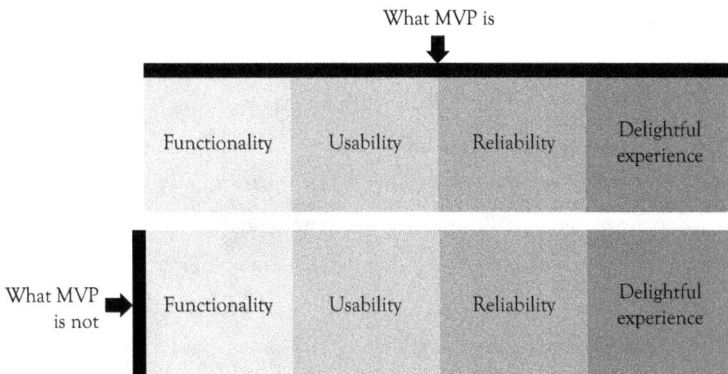

Figure 7.7 What an MVP is and what it is not

An Example of MVP failure

When I worked in a digital banking department, I was designing an instant loan platform for small e-commerce businesses. Traditionally, when the owner of an e-commerce business wants to obtain a loan, they contact a relationship manager. The relationship manager asks them to supply paper documents (e.g., incorporation certificate, financial reports from the last three years) to evaluate the business viability and profitability. They then decide whether or not the customer should be granted a loan and how much the loan amount should be. The problem for the customer was that the process was manual and time-consuming. The customer needed to meet the relationship manager, deal with all the paperwork, and typically wait one month from the initiation of the request to get money in their account. Second, 70 percent of small e-commerce businesses are only one or two years old and would not have three years' worth of financial reports. What they did have to provide evidence of their business records were transactions on the e-commerce platform. But the bank's risk assessment process was rather rigid and it did not have a risk-assessment algorithm to process these transaction data. At that time, my team's idea was to provide a digital platform via which small business owners could submit loan applications based on their transactions. They would obtain instant results on the application and get the loan disbursed in their bank account within 24 hours.

Our team started to break down the components into two large categories: a digital experience and a reliable underwriting algorithm. We presented the solution idea and, since the bank did not have an algorithm that could process data other than historical financial reports, we suggested partnering with an external financial technology provider. Our team's suggestion was to build an MVP that would provide enough of a digital experience to the customer. It would include an algorithm that would manage the percentage of bad loans under a percentage similar to the current small business loan portfolio.

The plan was to test it for six months and evaluate the pilot result. The management team was relatively risk-averse and very concerned about the algorithm, even though there was a contractual clause that protected the bank, including the cosharing of loss and a guarantee from the FinTech to absorb losses beyond the agreed level. The decision was to pilot the algorithm first and since digital experience is relatively easy to build, it would be catered for in the next phase. The pilot was constructed in such a way that the customer would fill in a simplified, physical application form and submit it with three months' worth of historical data downloaded from the e-commerce site. The result of the loan application would be available in one week. If approved, the loan would be disbursed to them within one day. It shortened the turnaround time from four weeks to just one. Does that sound good enough?

What we did not know was that we were heading for a total failure. Some 12 weeks into the pilot, we'd only received a handful of applications. The response rate from customers was extremely low. Even customers who had applied once never returned. We were devastated and the management questioned the market demand for such a product. We decided to talk to customers to find out why.

We approached some customers who were offered the pilot but did not make a submission. We sat them down in a focus group and asked them why. One customer asked us, "If you are still asking me to fill in a form, what is the difference from the old application method?" Another customer said, "I am operating an e-commerce site and you expect me to download the data in a paper format? Why wouldn't you have a digital way of getting my data?" We tried to explain that we set out to test the algorithm first and in the next phase, include the digital experience. The customer replied, "The one thing that I wanted from this product was to get an instant loan digitally. Did your algorithm test help me with that?"

We were embarrassed to hear these comments but they spoke the truth. When we defined our MVP in this project, we focused too much on what we, as the bank, wanted to test, instead of what our customers needed. The MVP was broken and did not live up to the vision we had set. In short, we'd made a huge mistake in coming up with an MVP that did not meet the expectations of customers. When we rethought what the customers actually wanted, it was just a simple

(*Continues*)

(Continued)

> way of applying for a loan that gave them instant approval and money in the bank.
>
> Shortly after the meeting, we called off the pilot. We went back to the whiteboard and revised the MVP definition. We made it an end-to-end digital process for customers with minimal core features including an application page, back-end algorithm, and result page. We relaunched another MVP version one month later and it was a hit.
>
> Remember that each MVP launch is a learning opportunity. It is, of course, a win if your MVP hits the ground running and receives good feedback. But even if it does not work, try to understand why from your customers and improve your offering. This is what the MVP is designed for—launch and learn.

How to Define Your MVP

To define your MVP, you can start by breaking down the big idea into components. Combined with the validation results you have obtained in the problem-solving phase, you should be able to prioritize the components of your MVP. Here is a four-step guide on how you can define your MVP:

1. Referring to your customer journey, what are your customer's goals?
2. List their pain points by the level of pain.
3. Using 1 and 2 above as a reference and the 2×2 MVP features prioritization matrix later, layout the proposed features based on the level of impact and urgency.
4. Prioritize the features.

Figure 7.8 provides a framework for intrapreneurs to prioritize features for an MVP.

MVP launch is not about building the perfect version but it should provide a good-enough solution that addresses the customer pain points. For backend operations, it might be challenging to have all functions fully developed and integrated for the first launch. As long as it is assembled in a way that the key functions are fulfilled and it does not jeopardize the customer experience, it is a go. Remember, you can always get feedback and pivot after you launch the MVP.

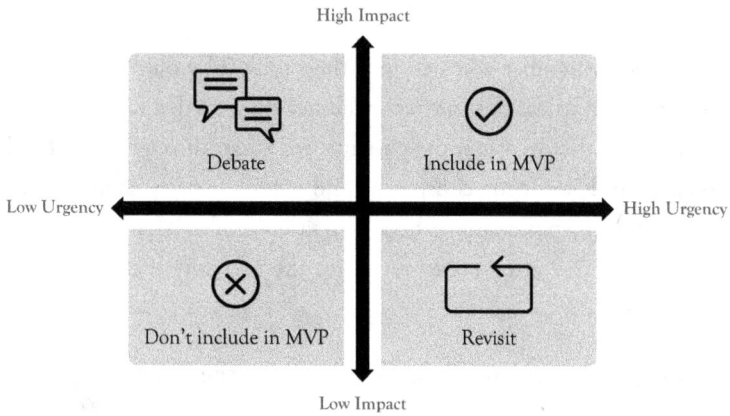

Figure 7.8 MVP features prioritization matrix

Intrapreneurship in Action: Defining MVP of PillPack

To illustrate how MVP and design thinking can be applied in solving a problem and building a product, let's look at an example focused on a pharmacy problem. The example demonstrates how the methodology helps progress the idea in each phase. This is a real-use case, while some of the information that describes how the methodologies are applied is based on my interpretation as a practitioner.

Background

TJ Parker worked at his parent's pharmacy when he was a teenager. Patients would visit the pharmacy with prescriptions from their doctors.[9] There were usually long queues inside the pharmacy as most patients needed to visit physically to get the medication. TJ would help pack or refill the medication for the patients according to their prescription.

Empathize

TJ observed that various types of medication were prescribed, each with different consumption frequencies (e.g., twice a week, three times a week, taken in the morning, and taken after lunch). To help

(Continues)

(Continued)

customers remember when to take their pills, TJ would write on the medication bottles. But to check whether they needed to take a medicine at a particular time, the patients had to go through every bottle to confirm. It was time-consuming and made the patients insecure.

Using TJ's observation, here is a sample of a patient's empathy map. Figure 7.9 attempts to mock up the empathy map of PillPack target customers.

Building Domain Knowledge and Forming the Team

On his journey to solving the problem, TJ trained as a pharmacist, obtaining a Doctor of Pharmacy (PharmD) degree from the Massachusetts College of Pharmacy and Health Sciences. Despite his strong domain background, TJ did not go solo. He met Elliot, an associate at Founder Collective and cofounder of MIT's Hacking Medicine program. Elliot was an engineer by training and a passionate advocate of customer-centered health care. TJ and Elliot partnered up and set sail on their journey.

Frame the Problem Statement

Based on the insights gathered from patients in the pharmacies and the empathy map, the problem statement could be something like this:

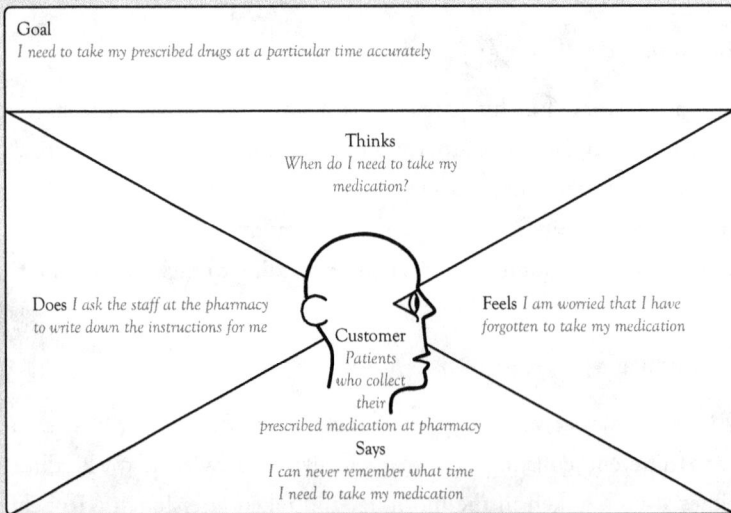

Goal
I need to take my prescribed drugs at a particular time accurately

Thinks
When do I need to take my medication?

Does *I ask the staff at the pharmacy to write down the instructions for me*

Feels *I am worried that I have forgotten to take my medication*

Customer
Patients who collect their prescribed medication at pharmacy

Says
I can never remember what time I need to take my medication

Figure 7.9 Sample of an empathy map

"As a patient who has to take multiple prescription medications, I want a simple way to keep track of what I should consume at different times."

Validating the Problem

TJ took what he'd observed and synthesized the problem statement. Then he needed to validate whether the problem was real. Based on his work at the pharmacy, he talked to patients about the issue. On top of that, TJ and Elliot also researched the fact that 30 million U.S. adults (that's one in 10) take more than five prescription medications a day.[10] By gathering customer feedback and macro data, the problem as defined was validated.

Ideate

To start the ideation phase, the conversion of the problem statement into the "How might we?" statement could look like this:

How might we design a solution such that patients who need to obtain or refill their medication based on a prescription from their doctors have a simple way to keep track of what they should consume at different times?

TJ started to brainstorm possible solutions to this problem. The potential ideas included:

- A widget that reminds the patient about the meditation
- An application that reminds patients about the medication and reduces confusion
- A smart pillbox for patients to plan their meditation ahead of time
- Packing the drugs for customers each day and sending them the medication

Some of the ideas got invalidated, including the widget, the reminder application, and the smart pillbox, because the problem was more complex than those solutions could solve. TJ and Elliot decided

(Continues)

(Continued)

to focus on building an online pharmacy that delivers drugs to patients in per-dose packets.

Define and Launch the MVP

The online pharmacy was not a small idea to execute. TJ and Elliot had to break down the components of such a huge platform. To make the idea work, bring the best experience to customers, and start the business, you can imagine the numerous features and capabilities the team would have to explore, including:

- User-friendly packaging design
- Automatic medication labeling
- An efficient overnight delivery system
- Powerful software platform that takes care of subscription, logistics, and customer database

TJ and Elliot finally launched the solution, PillPack, in 2013 but it was nothing like the idea described above. TJ mentioned in an interview with Founder Playlist that in the early days of the venture, his team would buy plastic food containers from Chinese distributors and blue decals from a printing shop in Cambridge.[11] They would ship 200 or 300 boxes a week and every Wednesday night, the team would spend six hours assembling them. They would manually cut openings into boxes so that patients could pull out the packs when they received them. They launched the product purely to get feedback from customers. That was PillPack's MVP.

Pivot and Scale Upon MVP Launch

After rounds of pivoting, TJ, Elliot, and their team revised the product based on market feedback and upgraded several capabilities thanks to the investment they'd secured. Today, PillPack offers customers:

- Personalized roll of presorted medications, convenient dispenser, and any other medications that cannot be placed in packets, such as liquids and inhalers.

- Medication label with a picture of each pill and notes on how it should be taken.
- Real-time notifications and an online dashboard for customers to control their shipments, refills, and copays. Customers can also e-mail, text, or call their PillPack pharmacist at any time to ask questions or clarify instructions.
- Best-in-class experience supported by PharmacyOS, a software platform that helps manage each customer's medications, coordinate refills, and renewals, and ensure that each shipment is sent on time, every time.

PillPack is licensed nationwide in the United States. From its launch in 2013 to 2015, it shipped more than 5 million packets of medication. In 2019, PillPack was acquired by Amazon at a valuation of $753 million.[12]

Agile Project Management

Intrapreneurs need to learn to manage the execution of ideas. In "Disciplined Innovation," you gained insights into how to break down big ideas into activities. Next, you need to plan the activities and make progress to push the idea forward. You need to build momentum and execute swiftly. If you are lucky, you might have a partner who is a professional certified project manager on your team to implement the project management approach. If not, there are quick tools and hacks for learning and managing it by yourself.

Traditionally, large corporations use the "waterfall approach" to manage projects. Once the project scope is confirmed, the project manager lays out the tasks from start to finish and assigns owners to execute them. Most workflows are linear and sequential. The waterfall approach is appropriate for large-scale projects with well-defined requirements and expected outcomes of high certainty. Since it involves extensive planning with sequential execution, the room for change in scope is limited and flexibility is low.

For intrapreneurs developing a new solution who want to move quickly, other approaches are required. Agile project management, which breaks down big projects into smaller parts, is more suitable for managing innovation. Agile focuses on constant and frequent deliverables. There is a strong focus on execution via collaboration. You might know agile as an approach for software development but, in fact, it is a methodology and mindset that can be applied across different types of innovation projects. In this section, we will cover the common agile methods and tools that can help you move your project forward. By learning it, you can apply agile to manage the progress of your design thinking and MVP activities.

Moving With Speed Using Sprint

Agile makes progress using a Sprint approach. Sprint is a time-bounded period in which the team sets for themselves to deliver a defined scope of work. Instead of managing a project over six months with 100 tasks, Sprint sets a specific scope of work ranging from one to four weeks. During a Sprint, the team agrees on the key tasks for delivering the relevant results during that period. Once they have completed that particular Sprint, the team comes together to evaluate the outcomes, including what is done, what is not, and what they want to focus on in the upcoming Sprint.

The team can decide how long a Sprint should be. The typical practice is to start on a Monday and end on a Friday. If it is a two-week Sprint, it starts on a Monday and ends on Friday the following week, with a total of 10 workdays in between. Using a Sprint to manage tasks and progress keeps the team focused and provides clarity on the priority of tasks. It also builds momentum for the team since the milestones are set in the near term in a manner that's achievable. It is not a good idea to have too long a sprint (anything beyond four weeks) as it's supposed to be fast moving.

Scope-Setting Using Sprint

Scoping is the first step in a Sprint. You and your team need to define the tasks you are onto. To achieve the agreed scope, the team has to collectively determine:

- What is the goal of this Sprint? Validate some key assumptions, test the feasibility of some features, come up with a high-level business model, and so on.
- What are the tasks involved? Based on the goal, what activities do you need in this Sprint?

- What are the target deliverables of each task? Decide what outcomes the team wants to achieve at the end of the Sprint.
- Who can carry out the work? Which team members are available for this Sprint?
- Who should work on what? Based on the skills of the team members, who would lead and/or partner together to complete which task?

Scrum Meeting With Kanban Visual

Setting up regular touchpoints with the team during a Sprint is important as all team members should be aware of any progress and roadblocks. One of the most efficient ways to keep track of the project progress is to set up a 5 to 10 minute standup or scrum meeting with your team, either in-person or virtually. The meeting frequency depends on the maturity of the project, for example, once per week for an early-stage idea or daily for a project in flight. To facilitate the meeting, you can use a Kanban board.

Kanban was developed in the 1940s by Taiichi Ohno, an industrial engineer and businessman working at Toyota Automotive. It was created as a planning system to control and manage work and inventory at every stage of production in an optimum manner.[13] A Kanban system takes care of the entire value chain, from sourcing raw materials to manufacturing to delivering the goods to customers. Much later, in 2004, David J. Anderson, a veteran of the software industry, started to apply the Kanban method to the field of information systems and software development. Kanban has since been applied as a method of tracking progress in various types of projects, or basically anything for which you would like to see gradual progress. One of the most commonly used tools of the Kanban method is the Kanban board. I have been using the Kanban board to track project progress and, over time, I have found that the simplest version works the best and can be applied to various types of projects. Figure 7.10 is a template of the Kanban board.

Bring the Kanban board into the meeting to visualize progress. Each meeting should be run in a way that everyone gets the chance to share the following:

1. What have you done?
2. What are you doing?

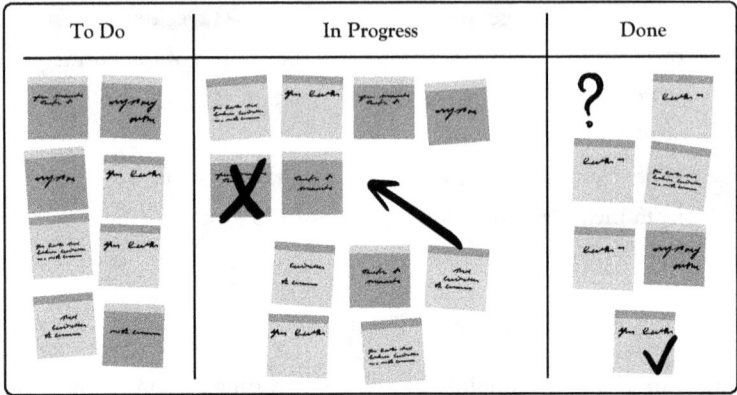

Figure 7.10 Kanban board

3. What else do you plan to do?
4. Is there any roadblock that you face?

The primary objective of this standup meeting is to provide a quick update on team activities, not to deep-dive into any task. If there is a roadblock, the team should quickly identify items for action or escalation. Anything that cannot be resolved in this 10-minute meeting should be followed up in a separate setting with the appropriate stakeholders.

Intrapreneurship in Action: Airbnb Team Built Online Experiences in Just 14 Days[14]

Intrapreneurship plays a critical role in business success, especially during turmoil when a big change is required within a short time. Airbnb was a good example. In 2020, the travel industry was impacted by the pandemic. Borders were closed and travels were restricted to stop the spread of the virus. Businesses in the airline and hospitality industries were at risk. Airbnb's business, which is dependent on traveling activities, was inevitably affected. One of the products,

Experience Worldwide, which offers guests in-person experiences, has experienced a significant decline due to the limitation of in-person activities. The program was put on pause to keep its hosts and guests safe. It does not affect Airbnb alone, but also the hosts who rely on the income generated from the program.

The Experience team who is in charge of the product was on to an urgent task to explore alternative revenue channels. Proactively listening to the hosts, the Experience team has observed the need for a new product for virtual experiences. The team started to collaborate with cross-functional teams including engineering, product, design, content, operations, marketing, and research.

To manage the project in a highly efficient manner, they have used:

- A project kickoff to solicit input from a broad range of stakeholders;
- Daily standups to ensure alignment across teams;
- Project tracker to visualize the work and help identify roadblocks; and
- Extensive testing by launching early and often.

The team has built an end-to-end product called Online Experience in just 14 days. It allowed them to support their host community while continuing to provide the guests with unique opportunities to stay connected during difficult times.

The product was a great success. Hundreds of thousands of guests around the globe have signed up for Online Experience. The initiative has transformed Airbnb's business model and expanded its business with a new income channel.

Map Your Internal Stakeholders

To strategize how to push an idea forward, you will need to think about the people in the organization who can support you, as well as those you need to spend the effort to convince if you anticipate pushback. Mapping

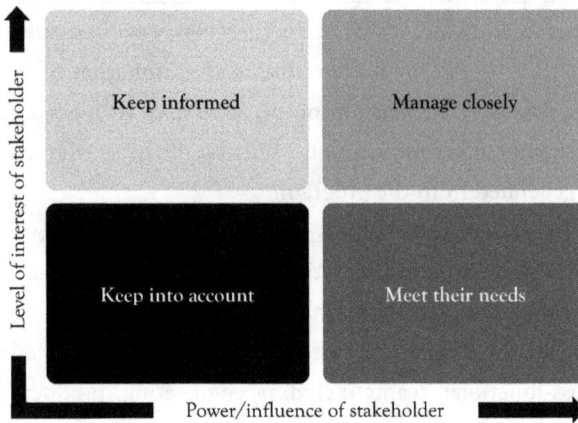

Figure 7.11 Stakeholder map

your internal stakeholders helps you visualize the motivations of different people, their level of interest in your idea, and the role they play in your plan. Start mapping stakeholders right from the start of a project and review it periodically. This is not project material that you would show to your stakeholders. It is a confidential document only to be shared among a small number of core team members. Figure 7.11 is the template of the internal stakeholders map.[15]

Keep Track of Decisions

A decision log is equally important for managing a big project or an early-stage idea. During the process of exploration, observations and validations result in decisions on which path to pursue. Along the way, more stakeholders come to the table and, based on their feedback or input, the direction of your idea might have changed or been adjusted. You will need to keep track of all those changes and the rationale for the decisions. This is to avoid back and forth arguments or overlooking information after a couple of months when no one remembers what was said and why a particular decision was made. Intrapreneurs should get into good habits by tracking decisions when the idea is in the development phase. The minimum you should do is write up a short minutes document after each meeting, with clear decision points and contributors. These should be shared with everyone involved in the meeting and the project.

#	Decision title	Decision details and rationale	Date	Who agreed?	Who needs to be informed?	Resulting action

Figure 7.12 Decision log template

A recommended approach is to keep a decision log, a document that records all the critical decisions made throughout the exploration of the idea and the project. A well-maintained decision log will help to:

1. Eliminate ambiguity and misunderstanding about a decision.
2. Inform members who are not present in the meeting.
3. Save time recalling who said what and why.

A good decision log should include information describing the issue discussed, the decision made, the time it is made, who agreed to it, the rationale it is based on, and the relevant action item (Figure 7.12). It might only take you two minutes to keep track of each decision. You might find it tedious to diligently maintain such a log but, believe me, you will find it very handy when you need to refer to it.

Leadership

Leadership was very different 20 years ago. With digitalization, technology advancement, and the exponential growth of social media, businesses today are facing a rapid pace of change. Leadership skill requirements have also been evolving. A leader is no longer simply a person who has direct authority over others. In fact, what the world needs today is effective leadership that is more of a mentality than a title. Anyone can lead effectively, even without authority, if they have developed the right skills. Obviously, there are many important skills in the domain of leadership. This section will focus on those that intrapreneurs should develop to achieve success in bringing innovation to their organizations.

Lead by Influence, Not Authority

Leadership is a choice you make rather than a place you sit. In other words, leadership comes from influence and not from your position. For this reason, even when you're not in front, you're still leading those around you.

—John Maxwell

As an intrapreneur, you have to collaborate widely with a diverse group of people. Most of those do not report to you. If you are in a senior position, you might be able to flex your muscles and apply your authority. However, that might not work all the time, especially with people who are sitting outside of your reporting verticals. The good news is that intrapreneurs don't need to rely on authority to lead. Leadership by authority is rigid and is not the best way of encouraging collaboration. People follow authority because they have to, not because they want to.

To lead without authority, you need to work on three things: building trust, seeking alignment, and creating vision.

- *Building trust.* Build your brand and reputation and let people who have worked with you advocate for you. You can achieve this by (1) delivering excellent quality of work, (2) demonstrating high integrity, and (3) building a sincere relationship with your work partners.
- *Seeking alignment.* Find the common ground between you and different work partners. Find out your common key performance indicators or how your idea would benefit them. Understand what your stakeholders want and always think of what you can offer them. Refer to "Stakeholders Management" under "Navigating a Large Organization" in this chapter.
- *Creating vision.* Have a clear vision of what you want to achieve. Apply storytelling to share the purpose of your idea and illustrate how bringing your ideas to life impacts the world and your customers. Refer to "Storytelling" under "Communications" in this chapter.

Questions for intrapreneurs:

- What is your leadership style?
- Have you met an influential leader who led without authority in your organization?

Lead Through VUCA

We live in a time of unpredictable changes and a rapid pace of change. Digitalization, Industry 5.0, and the pandemic are just three examples of this. So how can leaders of all kinds navigate an uncontrollable environment such as the one that exists in business today? One tool that has been gaining popularity is called VUCA. The concept of VUCA was coined by the U.S. Army in the 1990s to describe the post–Cold War world at that time in terms of four factors: volatile, uncertain, complex, and ambiguous.[16]

- *Volatile (V)*. Change is rapid and dynamic.
- *Uncertain (U)*. The future is hard to predict.
- *Complex (C)*. Factors for consideration are many and they are interconnected.
- *Ambiguous (A)*. Information is too incomplete to draw any conclusion.

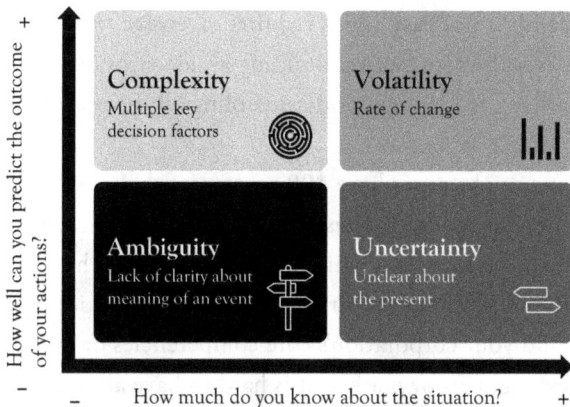

Figure 7.13 Dimensions of VUCA

The importance of leadership through VUCA has been emphasized to entrepreneurs and leaders in large corporations. But intrapreneurs also face their own set of VUCA challenges during the process of innovating for their corporations:

- *V*: Customer behaviors are changing rapidly. Their expectations are shaped by the experiences brought to them by innovative companies like Facebook, Google, Uber, and Airbnb. The industry that your corporation operates in is likely to have intensified competition from startups and other tech giants that are expanding into the field. Coupled with that, technological advancement is happening at a high speed which makes newer and better solutions more readily available.

- *U*: No one can predict when your business will be disrupted. There is no guarantee that the competitive advantage your corporation has today will still be there tomorrow. When you work on a new idea, a new market, or a new business model, it's always uncertain whether or not it will be a success before it is launched.

- *C*: Navigating a large organization is complex. You will need support from a wide group of people to get it over the line. There are also strategies, risks, and regulations that come into play. Understanding a complex problem in depth is not easy and it requires extensive research to discover the root causes. Building an idea from scratch, deploying technology, and assembling all the pieces are not simple tasks.

- *A*: You might never have 100 percent of the information before you call for a decision, whether it is deciding which problem to focus on, which idea to explore, or how to form the MVP for the first launch. When your idea goes beyond your corporation's core competencies or targets a new segment or market, it is hard to have all the data available.

Given all of the aforementioned, intrapreneurs should build on the four areas to successfully navigate VUCA:

- *See opportunity in each change.* Even the most drastic change brings new opportunities. During the pandemic, a lot of people had to work from home or in a kind of hybrid mode between the office and home. This posed challenges to operating businesses without disruption. Food and Beverages (F&B) and retail businesses have taken a strong hit with lockdowns and social distancing rules. The cessation of traveling impacted airlines, hotels, and travel agencies. The pandemic had a wide adverse impact across various industries, small businesses in particular. In mid-2020, research by McKinsey & Company showed that between 1.4 million and 2.1 million U.S. small businesses could close permanently as a result of the first four months of the pandemic.[17] This problem wasn't just confined to the United States, with businesses in Europe, Asia, the Middle East, and Africa encountering the same issues. However, even in the darkest times, there are opportunities. Amid the slow economic growth, the pandemic led to a surge in e-commerce and accelerated digital transformation. The share of global retail trade for e-commerce rose from 14 percent in 2019 to about 17 percent in 2020.[18] Companies operating online delivery, virtual meetings, and digital tools have benefited from the change in consumer behavior. Perhaps the most famous example is Zoom, a video conference tool. Its number of daily users rose from an average of 10 million worldwide in December 2019 to 300 million in April 2020. The company's share price rose ninefold, from $62 in April 2019 to $559 in December 2020. Volatility provides opportunities. It is not easy to navigate but it offers chances for people who stay on top of trends and are willing to look around for signs.
- *Keep up with innovation and technology.* The world is uncertain with all of the ongoing changes. To bridge the gap between problem and solution, you need to keep yourself updated with emerging technology trends and innovations

in the market. One of the traits of intrapreneurs is constant learning. Thanks to news and social media advancements, access to information is fast and easy. You can keep up with the latest changes by visiting sites like TechCrunch and WIRED, subscribing to innovation newsletters, and listening to podcasts relevant to your industry.

- *Move with agility.* Agile is mentioned under "Project Management" in this chapter. In fact, agile is more than a project management skill. It is a mindset that you can apply to navigate VUCA. Based on Henna Inam, author of *Wired for Disruption*, employees need to become catalyst leaders with four types of agilities:[19]

  1. *Context-setting agility:* You need to scan the environment, anticipate what might change, and frame the context in a compelling way that influences others.

  2. *Stakeholder agility:* You need to identify, seek out, and engage key stakeholders for input and alignment. Stakeholders have both the power to help you succeed or cause you to fail. Knowing the motivation of the stakeholders can help carry you toward your goal. Refer to "Stakeholder Management" under "Navigating a Large Organization"

  3. *Creative agility:* You need multiple views when dealing with a complex problem and to step back to examine the assumptions being made. You need to be able to get in-depth into the problem and yet expand your creativity to try ways of solving it without getting stuck.

  4. *Self-leadership agility:* You need to engage deeply in growing your self-awareness by first envisioning the kind of leader you want to be. There might not be a clear assignment that tasks you with solving the problem. You need to be self-driven and be able to motivate others to partner with you with self-leadership, not assigned leadership.

- *Be comfortable making decisions without complete information.* During the process of innovation, you will not be able to get all the data before you move on to the next stage. First, always verify the source of information to ensure you are making decisions based on factual and accurate information, even if it is not complete. Second, you need to synthesize all the information on hand and review its implications. Understand which piece of information is missing that you wish to have and analyze how much effort and time are required to find that missing piece. Most often, it is not realistic to wait until the data are complete. In that situation, intrapreneurs need to know how to break down the assumptions behind the decisions and move quickly to test them. Decide what parameters you need to measure to validate whether your decision is the right one and find a way to measure them. These parameters can include customer signup, retention, throughput rate, transaction uptake, and so on, depending on what the decision is. Once a decision is made and executed, observe the outcomes of the parameter in a timely way and respond or pivot if required.

Network Widely and Across Disciplines

Networking is an important skill for entrepreneurs as they venture into the unknown—they cannot be experts on everything and they need to tap into the resources of their network. If anything, networking is even more important for intrapreneurs because office politics comes into play. However, some people are hesitant when it comes to networking. It might seem like they are asking for favors or else they are not comfortable talking to people they don't know.

In fact, networking is about building relationships. It shows your sincere curiosity about other people. Networking should never start with your desire to get something out of the relationship. It starts with a simple and genuine thought that you are interested in someone else's story. And when you approach networking outcomes, you should always think first of what you can share or give rather than ask for. People tend to withdraw if your first goal of networking is selling or asking for help.

Many people in corporations view networking as a tool only for job hunting or getting their next assignment. That is, after all, the conventional way people harnessed their network. For intrapreneurs, though, the real impact of networking is far more than that.

How Can Intrapreneurs Benefit From Networking?

- *Inspiration.* Innovation can happen when you connect the dots across trends in different industries and fields. An application that works in one domain might be transferrable to others. Building a diverse network can help you widen your lens and draw inspiration from interacting with others.
- *Domain expertise.* Depending on the problem or solution you are working on, you should build a network with people who have a strong understanding of the domain. They have extensive insights based on their first-hand experience of the issues and they might also have made attempts to solve the problem but have not been able to. The sharing of learnings could be invaluable.
- *Sponsorship.* For an idea to take flight in an organization, intrapreneurs have to seek sponsorship from the management and relevant stakeholders. Networking with them helps you understand what motivates them and how you can better align with their thinking, increasing your chances of getting their support.
- *Intrapreneurial rapport.* Intrapreneurship is a process that requires persistence to steer through. Having a network of other intrapreneurs, inside or outside of your own organization, can help build a rapport system. You can exchange best practices and learnings along the journey.

Who Should you Build Your Professional Network With?

Networking is an investment of effort and time. Cast your net wide but, at the same time, try to prioritize as you need the energy to build new networks and maintain existing ones. Consider having the list of people below as your networking targets:

- Stakeholders in your corporation
- Other intrapreneurs in your corporation
- Cross-industry innovators or intrapreneurs

- Innovation consultants
- Subject-matter experts
- Startups that are working on similar problems
- People who have experience with the technology you are exploring for the solution

How Do you Build and Expand Your Network?

If you have been working in the same corporation for a long time, you might find your network becomes confined to your own department or team over the years. It is easy to fall into the trap of only connecting with the people you work with. There is nothing wrong with building a strong and deep network with your co-workers. But you might be missing the opportunity to widen your perspective as people who work around you tend to have similar thinking processes and shared knowledge of the same domain. You should try to expand your network. Below are some great places for intrapreneurs to network beyond their team:

- Reconnect with your old network—people who have made a career change or are no longer in your current circle.
- Attend internal town hall and corporate sharing sessions.
- Volunteer for an internal task force or think-tank.
- Attend industry and technology conferences and connect with the speakers and attendees.
- Sign up as a speaker at events to share your knowledge.
- Volunteer at industry events.
- Be a committee member of an industry group.

In my personal experience, I have found that the more you give, the stronger the network you can build from that engagement. An example of a network I benefited from was the internal digital task force for which I volunteered when I was working as a relationship manager in my early career. That was not part of my job scope. The digital task force was formed in the early days of digital transformation and, at that time, I did not know much about technology. It was an unofficial group in which some employees volunteered to imagine and brainstorm ideas that could benefit the future of the bank. By participating in the group,

I forged close bonds with people who shared the same passion for digital transformation. With all the knowledge shared among members, I gained insights into exciting trends and learned a lot within a short timeframe. The network carried me a long way and some of the co-workers I met in the group became good friends.

Another example is Women in FinTech Singapore, a networking platform under the Singapore FinTech Association. I have a strong interest in the FinTech scene in Southeast Asia and I started to attend FinTech events when I relocated to Singapore. From the group, I built an extensive network of people working in the field. Later, I decided to become a committee member of the group to drive engagement. The group allowed me to stay close to industry progress and also meet interesting people who widened my horizons.

The main takeaway is that you should find out which professional networks you would like to engage with. If you have an interest in that group, start by participating in events, getting to know the team, and if you are keen, considering whether you can contribute or play a role such as becoming a committee member. If you're short of time to commit too much, you can still stay close and build your network from it.

Getting Comfortable With Virtual Networking

Since the start of the pandemic, meeting people in person has been challenging. Many industry conferences, seminars, and roundtables have gone online. Besides these events, people have also been shifting their professional networking to virtual settings. Even if our normal, in-person lifestyles resume postpandemic, virtual networking is here to stay. But if you're facing a challenge building a network remotely, you are not alone. Instead of seeing virtual networking as a second-best option, try to leverage social media and virtual tools. With the help of technology, you can break down geographical and timezone barriers to reach out to people around the world. These are things you can do to build your network virtually:

- *Follow groups on social media*: Research groups related to specific topics or industries on LinkedIn, Facebook, Clubhouse, Instagram, and so on. Since the start of the pandemic, many industry and technology groups have established a social media presence for marketing. Use keywords to search for the groups' pages. Start following them and subscribe to their mailing lists to stay on top of updates and events.

- *Postevent:* When you attend a webinar, roundtable, or conference, make a note of the speakers or panel members with whom you want to connect. If they have shared contact details, you can reach out by sending a note to them. Start by thanking them for their contribution to the event and say that you found the information helpful or inspiring. You can share that you have relevant experience and express your interest in connecting for a further deep dive on the topic. Because you have attended their session and find the topic relevant, the person is more likely to be open to connecting than a cold contact.

- *1-2-1 using LinkedIn*: Research people's profiles on LinkedIn. Identify people you find interesting, who have a similar career, or who are interested in a similar topic. Reach out to them with a note. Your note should be sincere and not too common like "Let's connect" or "Please add me to your network." Understand what you have in common, why you want to connect, and how connecting might benefit them. A good example could be: "Hi John, your professional network is very impressive. I am working as/aspire to develop myself as a [role]. Since you've been in a similar field, I would like to connect with you and hope we can exchange ideas." Do understand that LinkedIn outreach is always a probability game. Think how many people you replied to or connected with when you receive an invitation from a cold contact. Do not overthink it. Just do it and if it does not work, simply move on.

Navigating a Large Organization

One of the fundamental differences between an entrepreneur and an intrapreneur is the environment. Entrepreneurs are very much on their own, free to explore what they want to build using their business instincts. Intrapreneurs are, of course, working in large corporations. If navigated well, the corporation offers an excellent platform and resource for the intrapreneur to leverage. On the flip side, it could also create constraints and roadblocks that an entrepreneur in the outside world would never expect to deal with. Let's take a look at a few of the things intrapreneurs have to deal with.

Stakeholder Management

Entrepreneurs can start working on their own ideas based on their gut feelings or what their business instincts tell them the next big thing might be. They need no permission to start. Of course, the risks they take are high but they have the freedom to explore. This is not the case if you are an intrapreneur. To explore a new idea in a large corporation, you need to convince your stakeholders by finding alignment. You need to make sure what you are exploring is beneficial to your organization and that you are trying to make an impact on the business.

When I worked in the digital department at a regional bank, I met a wonderful mentor, Mok. At that time, Mok was the managing director of the community business portfolio. He was a sincere, humble, and approachable leader. Despite facing constant business challenges and having to stand up to other departments, he always found a way to resolve issues leaving everyone satisfied. He seemed to have the magic touch so I went to seek his advice. He did not lecture me on the topic. Instead, he told a story. That story has certainly changed the way I look at stakeholder management. I will share it with you now.

The Story of the 18th Cow

In a village, there was an old farmer who worked extremely hard to raise his family. He had three sons whom he loved dearly. After the farmer passed away, he left his sons 17 cows in his will. In his will, he'd written,

> I have decided to distribute my livestock in the following order. My eldest son shall get half of the livestock. My second son will get one-third of them. And my youngest son will have one-ninth. No cow should be harmed or partly owned.

The three sons tried to do the math. Half of 17, nor one-third or one-ninth makes a whole number. How could they divide the cows without killing them or owning part of a cow? They could not figure out how to resolve the problem but they did not want to go against the old man's last wishes. Since they could not decide what to do, they sought advice from the wisest man in the village. The wise man listened to their challenge. He thought about it for a while and said, "Bring your 17 cows here tomorrow and I will solve it for you."

The next day, the three sons went to the wise man's house with their 17 cows. The wise man was just arriving, having walked back from his neighbor's house with one cow that he'd borrowed. The wise man said, "Now with your seventeen cows and my one cow, there is a total of 18 cows. Let's see how I can make it work.

First, the eldest son gets half of 18 cows, which equals nine cows.

The second son then gets one-third, which equals six cows.

The youngest son will get one-ninth, which equals two cows.

Now that you have shared all 17 cows, I will take back the one cow I borrowed and return it to my neighbor."

All three sons were happy that the problem was solved. Everyone got what they were entitled to. No cow was harmed or partly owned.

So what does the story tell us about stakeholder management?

The three brothers were struggling with their father's instructions. Each was focused on what they were entitled to, based on their own motivation. The problem could not have been resolved if the three brothers had insisted on sharing the asset based only on what was written and the current scenario. They could have split the asset by killing the cows and taking the parts, which would have diminished the real value of what their father had left them.

However, stakeholder management is not a zero-sum game in which one gains and the other must lose. By bringing an additional cow, the wise man expanded the pie and made the sum of the cows dividable. He created an entirely different scenario in which the problem could be solved. Everyone could walk away with a satisfying result because he had created a win–win scenario. When facing stakeholder management issues, the challenge is finding "the eighteenth cow." What is "the eighteenth cow" in your scenario and how can you find it and present it to your stakeholders?

It could be strategic alignment, negotiated deals, future revenue, or an opportunity with mutual benefits. Articulate what is in it for stakeholders if they help you achieve your goal. The bottom line is that no one should be worse off by reaching an agreement, given their level of investment.

Dealing With the Corporate Immune System

If your idea is on the radical side and could cause disruption to the existing business, you should expect pushback. The corporation you work in has an existing hierarchy, policy, procedures, and system. It operates well together when the activities carried out are in line with what it is used to. Innovation is something new that the existing regime might not apply to. Like the human body, corporations have an immune system and the corporate immune system is fundamentally conservative.[20] It is there to provide stability and keep the organization running smoothly. It protects the organization from productivity disruption and gives most employees rules and routines to follow so that they provide reliable services to customers. When you are trying to push forward a new idea, you are pushing your corporation (including the management, your team, and the stakeholders involved) out of its comfort zone. When shaken, the immune system can perceive your idea as a threat. It then triggers a reaction to resist and neutralize the change, even though it might bring good results. This resistance can take various forms from resource retrieval, deprioritization, and a decision-making black hole, to political maneuvering.

Bootstrap During the Early Stage

Bootstrapping means building your idea using existing resources, without asking for additional funding or investment. Typically, you would be able to draw upon knowledge, skills, and person-hours. If you can find allies in the corporate who are interested in exploring the idea, the resource could be multiplied. This might sound weird. Why would you bootstrap like an entrepreneur while you ask for resources from within your corporation? The reason is that, depending on the culture and infrastructure, asking for funding does not always help the idea progress. The problem with corporate funding is that it might put your iterative, experimental approach in danger.[21] A rigid approach in a business environment can be harmful to early-stage ideas. It could sound outrageous if you ask for a half-million-dollar check. So as an intrapreneur, you need to be resourceful. Think through what you actually need as resources. In most scenarios, you only need two things: people and tools. People could be researchers, designers, prototypers, engineers, or domain experts. Tools could be the software, the technology, or the applications. Be specific about your ask and source them by going to the right people to support you to move forward. People might not have the money but they might bring along the skills and tools you need. That is if you can convince them of your idea and collaborate with them. Build traction and tangible outcomes by bootstrapping and use the outcome as leverage to build a solid pitch for increased investment.

Dealing With "You Are Eating My Pie"

In the open market, it's easy for entrepreneurs to launch products. If one of those products disrupts the market, the winner takes all. As with Darwin's law of evolution by natural selection, the fittest solution survives. But it is not that easy in a corporation. During my time working as a corporate innovation coach, I have seen the trigger of the corporate immune system at work. Most commonly, it was because a new idea had the potential to cannibalize the existing business. I have seen wonderful ideas that offer customers a better experience at low cost, with a good chance of being profitable, shut down because they might put existing products at risk. The existing products were not even good. They were clumsy, expensive to the customer, and gave them a poor experience. And yet people rallied to defend the product and hammered the new idea, even before it took shape. The emotional attachment to old products was strong. You'd usually hear defensive voices say things like:

- We have invested so much in the old product over the years.
- We have built a large team to support the old product's maintenance and customer service.
- Customers are used to the old product.
- The old product is still on par with our competitors.

- We can launch the new idea five years from now when the old product comes to the end of its life. By then, we would have earned enough from the old product.

As an intrapreneur caught in this situation, you would feel the tension, especially when the old product is backed by powerful and senior stakeholders. To push forward, you can try a few approaches:

- *Find your super anchor.* Identify influential leaders in the organization who embrace innovation and seek their buy-in. Make them advocates of your idea. Leverage them as strong anchors who can help you reach out to other stakeholders. They might be in a better position to convince other stakeholders to partner with you, given their relationships and network.
- *Try to partner with the resistant force.* First, find out what is the key business target of the people who are opposing your idea. They did not object to your idea for no reason. They might have felt the threat of losing their business. What if you make them the owner of the new product? That way, the revenue from your new product benefits their books. They would then have a stake in the idea and the motivation to make it successful. You might think that the credit is being taken away from you but you have to think bigger. Your career does not rely on one idea alone. The skills and capability you demonstrated during the execution will take you to your next venture. As an intrapreneurial talent, you might not want to create just one single product and be the owner of it forever.

Corporate leaders in charge of innovation strategy need to build a mechanism to resolve the conflict of cannibalism for the company's long-term growth. You can refer to Chapter 6, "Ideas That Might Self-Cannibalize" for more information.

So far, I have discussed the skills of intrapreneurs, including disciplined innovation, leadership, and navigating a large organization, earlier in this chapter. But there is one last essential skill an intrapreneur must have in order to solicit buy-in for their ideas: communication. Every successful intrapreneur is required to act as a salesperson when the time comes, to articulate the idea to others in a convincing way. By demonstrating strong communication skills, intrapreneurs can attract others to join their team, provide the team with investment, and provide management support to help them remove roadblocks like red tape. In the section below, I'll cover the advanced communication skills that intrapreneurs require.

Communications

Ability to Demystify Complex Concepts

Most people reject information that they do not understand. It makes them feel confused and stupid, which might trigger negative emotions toward the idea presented. As an intrapreneur, you are often dealing with complex problems. Sometimes the solution that you come up with can be highly technical or one requiring deep domain expertise. Technically, it can be extremely complicated. However, when you are selling your idea to stakeholders or explaining it to people outside of your core team, it should always be easy to understand. Do not assume that the audience has the same level of knowledge as you do. Do not expect them to know the jargon of your field. If you can break down a complex concept into something easily understandable, you will get more, and faster, buy-in. The last thing you want is for your brilliant idea to be undermined and discounted because the audience does not understand it.

Consider an intrapreneur in a bank who is trying to pitch an idea to detect fraudulent payments using artificial intelligence. Consider the following two ways of selling the same concept:

- Approach 1
  Our team is applying deep-learning techniques to predict fraudulent transactions made in the client's shared-service center. The learning is unsupervised, using structured and unstructured data relevant to the use case. Data processing throughput is 5,000 transactions per second. We trained the model using historical data from the last six months. Our model training followed the 80/20 rule. So far, our type I error rate is 2 percent.

- Approach 2

  Our corporate clients are processing hundreds of payment transactions every day. Among them, some transactions could be fraudulent. To stop those transactions quickly to avoid financial loss to our clients, our team is working on a solution using artificial intelligence. Our solution aims to detect fraudulent transactions and bring them to our clients' attention before they happen. This could potentially save $500,000 worth of losses per quarter due to fraudulent payments and the headcount we deploy to investigate these losses.

Which approach do you prefer as an audience? Which one do you find easier to understand and more relatable? The first approach is more presenter-centric. The presenter focuses on what they want to share with the audience and what they believe is important information based on their domain knowledge. The second approach is more audience-centric. The presenter takes care of what the audience wants to know and what is important for them to take away. When communicating a complex concept, the key is to adopt an audience-centric approach. Consider using the following techniques:

1. *Understand who your audience is.* Seek to know who the audience is in your setting. Do you know their level of knowledge and experience relevant to the topic? Do they understand the industry terms? Are they aware of the trends?

2. *Know what your audience cares about.* What does your audience really want to know? Depending on who they are, they might have different motivations. If they are in sales, mostly they'll want to know how your solution will increase sales opportunities. If they are strategists, they'll want to know how your solution fits into the company's three-year plan. If they are product teams, they'll want to know how your solution increases product revenue and how it integrates with existing product suites. Sometimes what you find the most fascinating part of your project could be totally irrelevant to the people you are presenting it to. Think about what is in it for them when you plan your pitch.

3. *Do not assume.* Imagine you have been working on the same problem and solution for the last couple of months and you know every bit of it. You get it. But your audience was not there in the laboratory with you. They have limited prior understanding of the issue, not a thorough understanding like you. Give them a sufficiently high-level, big-picture overview to begin with. If the audience mix is more generic, most likely they'll want to know the problem, the solution, and the benefits before they can deep-dive.

• *Avoid any jargon.* It's common for a highly complex business environment to have acronyms and terms related to particular domains. Most of us use them without thinking. It is important to replace jargon with plain language. Some audiences get lost after a few terms and lose interest. More engaged audience members will raise their hands and ask questions, but that will still interrupt your flow. Ask yourself whether the use of jargon is really necessary and whether it helps to convey the message. And 99 percent of the time, the answer is no.

Intrapreneurship in Action: Dreamworks—Hiring Experts That Can Talk to Laymen

Dan Satterthwaite, head of HR at Dreamworks, recognized that the work people do at the company was highly collaborative.[22] So much so that Dreamworks must employ people who not only sit at their desks and solve problems but can articulate the solution to their supervisor and team. Based on that requirement, the company has deep-dived into the recruitment process. It looks for people who not only are the best at what they do but can also communicate their ideas to others outside their field of expertise. Regardless of the type of job they are applying for, Dreamworks needs them to translate their knowledge into a language that others can grasp. During the recruitment process, the recruitment team asks questions about how the candidate solved a problem. The recruiters want them to be able to present that solution to a group of people who might not be in their domain, to test whether they can share their knowledge in a way that others can understand.

Product Storytelling

You can have a great product, but a compelling story puts the company into motion.

—Ben Horowitz, American entrepreneur and investor

Humans are drawn to stories. From fairy tales to Netflix movies, people have always enjoyed a good narrative. Well-crafted stories can lead to a change of emotions and help to connect people as if they were experiencing the story itself. You might have heard about corporations using storytelling in branding and marketing. The fact is storytelling also applies to business ideas. When you are pitching your idea, you want to get other people's buy-in and support. The more compelling and relatable the story is, the easier it is to convince your audience. Storytelling should not be viewed as a marketing gimmick. Instead, it should be used as a vehicle to share your mission and passion for the idea.

If you are used to selling ideas by product features and functions, you might struggle to come up with a story. The fact is you might have already known the story without realizing it. Each idea should have some linkage and relevancy to a customer's story. If you've followed the technique introduced under "Problem-Solving by Design Thinking," there's a good chance you have understood the users' perspectives and built empathy with them. To tell a compelling story, you can make use of the following steps:

1. *Build a character.* Use your customer to build your character in the story. Know your customer's persona. What are the person's characteristics, behavior, job, and goal? What does your customer's normal day look like?
2. *What's the tension or conflict?* What is your customer's unsolved problem or unarticulated needs? What is stopping your customer from achieving their goals? How do they feel about it? What is this problem costing them?
3. *Imagine the possibility.* What if the solution exists today? What does the ideal scenario look like? How would your customer feel about the problem being solved? How does it affect your customer's life or interaction with others?

Use real-life examples as much as possible and craft the story of your idea around its purpose. Don't ever lead into the story by stating, "Let me share a story with you." Do not even mention the word "story." Instead, make it real. If you happen to be one of the users of the product and are affected by the problem, use your own story to make it more personal and powerful.

Storytelling is a complementary technique to enhance the persuasiveness of your message. It helps create a strong impression of your mission and provides an emotional punch. Well-told stories will resonate with stakeholders, team members, and customers. It also makes it easier for people to retain information when it is told as a story. Despite that, beware of using storytelling alone. Without data and facts to support the commercials, it would not be sufficient to convince stakeholders, especially those who would invest resources in your idea. Learn to combine various communication techniques, and decide when and how to bring in a mix of relevant information for a good pitch.

Intrapreneurship in Action: Pampers Diapers Revolution

Victor Mills was 60 years old when he became a grandfather. At that time, in 1956, he had been working at Procter & Gamble (P&G) for 31 years.[23] Back then, diapers were made of cloth, which had to be washed. For new parents, it was a huge amount of work dealing with dirty diapers, coupled with sleepless nights taking care of a newborn. Diapers that weren't properly cleaned caused skin issues in babies and created stress for the parents. Plus, changing a cloth diaper was complicated and the task often fell upon women to perform.

Victor was trained as a chemical engineer and had spent his career working on consumer products at P&G. After his grandchild was born, he started to help with changing the diapers. He was unsatisfied with how the cloth diapers worked and hated washing nappies. He started to explore the idea of using shredded, absorbent paper in a nappy that could be disposed of after use. The early nappies Victor launched were very basic, essentially rectangular pads of tissue paper

(Continues)

(Continued)

> with a rayon liner and polyethylene outer. But with the launch of disposable diapers, more men could handle changing diapers for kids with minimal training.
>
> The disposable diaper is a wonderful story that came out of the love of a grandfather. It connected with thousands of families who were going through the important life stage of having a baby. In the marketing campaign, P&G also used the product to fight against social stereotypes by showing that men could change diapers too.

In this chapter, we have discussed the various skills required for intrapreneurs to be successful. They should be "comb-shape" talents who are good generalists but with the capability to go deep into various domains. They need to know how to innovate in a disciplined manner. They must be able to understand problems, master leadership skills, and be skillful communicators when pitching ideas and breaking down complex concepts.

As a leader, you first need to assess whether your employees possess these skills and where the gaps are. Every intrapreneur is unique in their skills and you need to help them form a development plan to upskill.

It is rare for an intrapreneur to be a master of all the skills and domain knowledge required to execute an idea on their own. Innovation will proceed much more efficiently if your intrapreneurs join forces and work together. In the next chapter, we will discuss the various types of intrapreneurs and how they work best as a team.

CHAPTER 8

Network of Diversity

Intrapreneurship isn't limited to specific types of people or roles. Intrapreneurs can come from different backgrounds and possess different domain skills. At the same time, intrapreneurship is typically not a solo activity. Along the way, people need to collaborate with, and seek knowledge from, others. To bring a big idea to fruition, you need a core intrapreneur team who can contribute in different areas, complement each other's skills, and divide and conquer.

As a corporate leader, you should identify which types of intrapreneurs you have and which are missing, and explore how to encourage collaboration among different types of intrapreneurs. Every intrapreneur has unique characteristics, expertise, skills, and experience. In this section, we will discuss avatars that help you define intrapreneurs in terms of their professions and characteristics. Professional avatars relate to an intrapreneur's educational background, training, and experience. On the other hand, character avatars relate to a person's personality and mentality.

The avatars described here are not exhaustive and are not intended for putting intrapreneurs in boxes. People can sit anywhere in the spectrum of avatars and can have different permutations of professional and character avatars. The categorization simplifies a host of factors to help you better understand yourself and others. Once you know this, it helps you find the right team, know the strength of team members, and understand how to work better with them.

Professional Avatars

Professional avatars are based on the intrapreneur's educational background, training, and experience. They reveal what matters to a person, what motivates them, what skills they bring to the team, and the roles they can play. There are five main professional avatars: the Business Venturer, the Academic Pro, the Design Guru, the Tech Hacker, and the Domain Specialist. These are not mutually exclusive avatars and, with appropriate training and experience, a person can possess a combination of different professional avatars.

Business Venturer

Business Venturers are people with strong business acumen. They understand how business works in the corporation: what the target market is, what drives revenue, and how the corporation makes a profit. Their business acumen can come from either education (a business degree or MBA) or experience. They have experience in leading a business within the corporation—a profit center like sales and marketing or a particular department or franchise. They know how to read the financials of a company. They have a strong sense of commercialization and understand how the business model works. They understand how external factors affect the business. They are good at creating the vision and strategy. Their domain expertise leans more toward strategy, product, and organization knowledge. Business Venturers are potential serial intrapreneurs as they constantly form ideas by reading changes in the market and the business. They draw inspiration from competitors, observations of customers, and reading the market.

Academic Pro

Academic Pros are people who have deep domain expertise in the subjects they study. They are expert innovators. They have usually earned PhDs and have done extensive research on the subject matter. A PhD not only masters the field but is also tasked to push the field forward by exploring new findings. Their research might have resulted in discoveries that can be applied to benefit the business. They possess strong problem-solving skills and are keen to apply analytical sense. They approach problems with solid logic and understand how to design experiments. They are aware of the applicable tools and methods of their subject matter. They are not afraid of dealing with complex problems with a high level of ambiguity as they've been well trained throughout their research. They understand how to analyze data and know-how to leverage it for decision making. They draw inspiration from their research work and the latest progress in their field.

Design Guru

Design Gurus are people who practice design thinking as a profession. They go by the title of product designer or design thinker. They have been trained in design thinking, user interface or user experience, industrial design, human-centric design, or service design. They are good at conducting field research and drawing insights for the design of people-centered products. They specialize in understanding users by developing personas and designing the customer journey. They create user flows, wireframes, and prototypes to effectively conceptualize and communicate detailed interaction behavior. They draw inspiration from studying users and understanding their pain points.

Tech Hacker

Tech Hackers are people with a technology background. They are usually software developers or engineers. They come from domains like computer science, computer engineering, analytics, data science, and artificial intelligence. They have a deep understanding of the capabilities of technology and are passionate about it. They have a strong experimental mindset and understand technology frameworks like agile. They can prototype a concept via programming within a short turnaround time. They possess a good understanding of databases, application services, technology architecture design, and application life cycle development. They draw inspiration from advancements in technology and the applications they observe or experiment with.

Domain Specialist

Domain Specialists are people who have earned professional licenses or are practitioners in their fields. These are the doctors, nurses, lawyers, physicians, surveyors, accountants, architects, pharmacists, or someone who has spent sufficient time in their industry. They have strong practical knowledge and experience. They have direct access to customers or have dealt with the problem area during their careers. They are close to the problem and therefore have a strong vested interest in solving it. They draw inspiration from their daily work, the problems that they observe during their practice, and their interaction with customers.

What Professional Avatar(s) Do you Need in Your Intrapreneur Team?

The Business Venturer and the Design Guru are common avatars since they provide skills that can be applied across problems and solutions. You should have these two avatars on your team. Next, depending on the problem and the solution you are trying to build, you will need different skills and hence a combination of different professional avatars in your team. For example, if you are working on a problem that involves changing the delivery of medicine in the health care system, you will need a domain specialist in the pharmacy industry to provide insights into the existing system. On the other hand, if you are working on solving a problem that involves a big breakthrough and you require deep knowledge and pioneering discoveries, you might need an Academic Pro. If the solution you are exploring involves software development, you will most likely need a Tech Hacker. Try to strategize the team mix by analyzing the skills you require.

Character Avatars

On top of professions and skills, another factor that affects the team dynamic is the character of people. In his book *Surrounded by Idiots*, Thomas Erikson, a behavioral expert, introduced his theory of the four types of human behavior.[1] He has observed people's behavior, identifying what motivates different people and understanding how they react.

Using this framework, you can understand how different character types affect the intrapreneur team, their strengths and weaknesses, and how the team can perform better. The four types of human behavior are Red, Yellow, Blue, and Green. Only about 5 percent of people have just one character avatar. You can be a combination of two or even more, and some people have a dominant avatar that can be easily observed.

The Red

The Reds are people who are highly driven, ambitious, and bold. They set high goals and strive to achieve them. They have a firm belief that they can achieve anything if they try hard enough. They enjoy challenges and react positively under pressure. They are competitive. They have a strong bias toward action and, in their mind, thought and action should happen at the same time.

In an intrapreneur team, Reds are good initiators and leaders. They are often good at setting direction and forming strategies. They can lead the team with their vision. They are decisive—not necessarily making the right decisions all the time but they nonetheless make a decision and move on. Having a Red on the team keeps the team focused on progress and builds strong momentum.

In terms of weaknesses, the Reds can be very dominant and therefore the team needs to make sure it balances the voices of different members. Reds can be impatient when progress is slow. Beware of their hot temper, which might put pressure on the team.

The Yellow

The Yellows are highly optimistic. They are very good at coming up with ideas and are not afraid of out-there thoughts. They often think outside the box and inspire the team. The Yellows are good visual thinkers. A Yellow can visualize things in their mind without actually experiencing them. They are cheerful and happy people to work with.

In the intrapreneur team, Yellows are often the ones with lots of ideas. Their contribution during the ideation stage is significant. They are very good storytellers and, in fact, most Yellows are good at selling. They can be the salesperson in the intrapreneur team to help pitch the idea. They are also great at networking as they can build relationships with a diverse group of people. They are natural collaborators.

Yellows might not be good at details and have little idea how to proceed to the next step. They are obsessed with high-level ideas but do not have a strong execution mindset. If you have a Yellow in the team, make sure that they come up with a plan and follow through. Do keep track of their progress from time to time to make sure things are happening.

The Blue

The Blues are extremely detail-minded. They focus largely on tasks and execution. They are perfectionists. They have high standards for their quality of work. They are data and facts oriented and demand high accuracy. The Blues are very organized and they always approach tasks with a plan. They care about order and logic. Spreadsheets and project planners are their favorite tools.

In an intrapreneur team, having a Blue is a valuable asset. The Blue is the one who gets your numbers right and thinks through the execution details, while the others are too excited about the new idea and the possibilities. The Blues are very realistic and practical. They are the ones who bring ideas back to Earth and work on them diligently, step by step. They spend extra hours ensuring that even the slightest details get sorted.

In terms of weaknesses, the Blues are relatively cautious and therefore might not buy into new ideas easily. You would have to present facts to convince them. If they cannot assess the risks of a new idea, they might refrain from starting it. Try to help the Blues get across the starting line by offering facts and analysis. Because the Blues are extremely detail oriented, they might sometimes miss the big picture. Do bring them back and remind them of the high-level objective from time to time. Blues tend to demand all the information before they can make a decision. You need to help Blue team members balance this tendency as it's impossible to be certain about everything in advance, especially in an innovation project. Blues are also not the loudest on the team but their opinions are usually well thought through. So do make an extra effort to encourage participation and seek input from them.

The Green

The Greens are the majority of people in the world. They are the average of all colors. They are the most balanced. They are calm, leisurely, and easygoing. They do their work as they are supposed to. They are good listeners and are very helpful to others. They are also good team players.

Having a Green on the team brings calmness and provides stability to the team when conflicts happen. They are reliable and deliver results according to the plan. They are usually friendly to work with. However, it's not often that you would have many Greens as intrapreneurs because Green does not like change in general. They do not have strong opinions about things and often do not take sides. Greens are also not too excited about new ideas. They do not see the urgency in most things. Given the characteristics of Green people, they are not the biggest fans of being in a team pushing for something new.

What Character Avatars Do you Need in Your Intrapreneur Team?

When forming your team, you will need to put together people who can help drive the idea forward. A team works best if it has people with all the character avatars so that you have a balanced team. While that might not be possible, you definitely want to have a Red to steer the direction, a Yellow to contribute and sell ideas, and a Blue to look after the plan and the details of execution. A Green might not be readily available since they do not like change. But if they are, they would provide good support for getting the work done. You also need to observe the dynamic between different character avatars for improving the efficiency of the team. In general, Greens work well with most people. Red and Blue usually work well together, with one setting direction and the other looking after tasks. Putting Yellow and Blue together is challenging as one talks at a very high level and the other is extremely detail oriented. If Yellow and Blue in the intrapreneur team work together, keep track of their progress and see if they need help communicating with each other.

Size of Intrapreneur Team: Not the More the Merrier

Every team should be small enough that it can be fed with two pizzas.
—Jeff Bezos, founder of Amazon

The size of the team matters when you are pushing an innovative idea forward. Of course, the more support you have, the better. But it does not necessarily mean having more core team members. Once the core team grows to a certain size, there is a trade-off between resources and speed. In his research work, Nis Frome surveyed over 300 decision makers to discover their most significant challenges and decision-making strategies.[2] One of the areas studied was the team size that contributes to the best outcomes. He found that almost nine in 10 respondents indicated that teams of two to five people made for the best decision-making process.

Innovation work is inherently uncertain and the pace of work is relatively fast. Having a small team allows decisions to be made swiftly and with autonomy. A small and nimble team ensures that people work closely and spontaneously. Since innovation involves ambiguity, having too many people results in too much deliberation, too much consensus, and too little actual progress. Try to limit your team to around five people and be clear about the role and expected contribution of each member. The other people who support the project are the stakeholders, who you keep informed.

When you move an idea forward, it is good practice to seek domain experts' input. Subject matter experts can help you understand existing ways of doing things, why things are done in such a way, and the current constraints they face. You need to collaborate with people who bring different expertise to the team. However, having too many experts can slow your project down. When the team is composed of a majority of experts, there is a tendency for team members to focus more on what they already know and less on exploring what they don't. They rely on the knowledge they've learned over the years and it takes them extra effort to unlearn it. Experts might, therefore, be limited by constraints known to them. They might be close to the domain knowledge but not necessarily close to the customer.

In her *Harvard Business Review* article, "Too Many Experts Can Hurt Your Innovation Projects," Riitta Katila revealed that innovation thrives when expert users make up about 40 percent of an invention team.[3] One of the reasons is that expert users have spent lots of time getting comfortable with existing tools and methods and can't always recognize a potential breakthrough innovation when they see one.

When you form your intrapreneur team, ensure that less than half of the members are experts. This is so that you have enough team members with no prior assumptions who can ask incisive questions. You do need subject matter experts and their input is valuable. But instead of having all of them on the core team, consider keeping some on an expert panel to tap into their knowledge from time to time.

In this chapter, we have introduced the different types of intrapreneurs. There are two ways of categorizing them: professional avatars and character avatars. Professional avatars tell you about the intrapreneur's training, educational background, and the skills they bring to the team. Character avatars tell you about the intrapreneur's personality, what motivates them, and how they work best with others.

Now you know how to team up your intrapreneurs to maximize the results of their efforts. But how can you attract intrapreneurial talents in the first place? What are intrapreneurs looking for when they join a corporate or a team? What motivates them to stay engaged and contribute their best to a company? And how can leaders effectively recruit and retain intrapreneurial talents? These are the questions we will focus on in the next chapter.

CHAPTER 9

Recruit and Retain Intrapreneurs

Tomorrow's workforce faces a world in which existing preconceptions do not apply.[1] With Industry 5.0, we are moving toward an era in which artificial intelligence, robotics, and the IoT will automate analytics, learning, and decision making. Given the changing dynamic of the relationship between people and work, leaders will have to rethink who they want to hire and how they retain the best talent.

Recruit Intrapreneurs

Know What Intrapreneurs Look Like

To recruit intrapreneurs, you first need to understand how to recognize them. In Chapter 3, we have discussed the traits of potential intrapreneurs. These traits will help you gain insights into a person's character and whether they have the right mindset. To embed this in your recruitment tools, use the questionnaire "The intrapreneur in you" in Chapter 2 to evaluate candidates. The questions are designed to assess the person's intrapreneurship traits and skills and the results will help you decide whether or not one particular candidate is more intrapreneurial than the others.

Identify Intrapreneurs During Interviews

To spot intrapreneurs, you should ask questions that reveal their intrapreneurial character and experience.

Problem Solving and Idea Implementation

- Can you share an example of a time you came up with, and implemented, a new idea for your company?

1. How did you approach the problem?
2. How did you come up with the idea?
3. Who did you liaise or collaborate with?
4. Can you share the process?
5. Who were the stakeholders and how did you manage them?
6. What was the result?
7. What were the learnings?

This set of questions helps you observe how the candidate approaches problem solving. Note the examples that the candidate discusses—ideas for new products, solutions, processes, and businesses are all relevant. Note how innovative the ideas are. How the candidate describes the process can give you insights into their mentality, for example, are they willing to try new ideas or do they stick with traditional ways of solving a problem? You should also find out about their innovation skills, including how familiar they are with innovation methodology, and their leadership skills for dealing with stakeholders.

Customer Obsession

- Can you tell us about a situation in which you had to deal with a difficult customer?

1. What was the situation?
2. What was the customer upset about?
3. What was the challenge?
4. How did you approach it? What actions were taken?
5. What was the result?

This set of questions will tell you how the candidate values customer relationships. Look for signs of empathy toward the customer. Can the candidate fully understand what the customer needs? Did the candidate go the extra mile to offer help? From the results, seek to look beyond the customer service aspect of the event. Look at the change the candidate brought to the organization based on this interaction with a customer. It is not just about calming an angry customer, but also about understanding what the candidate did to identify their unmet needs, and, based on this discovery, the action they took to change the product or service.

Handling Failure

- Can you share an experience of a failure you had at work?

1. What was the scenario?
2. What went wrong?
3. Who were the stakeholders involved?
4. What was the result?
5. How did you feel about the failure?
6. If you were to repeat the process, what would you change?

This set of questions tells you how the candidate handles failure. Some candidates are caught off guard facing this question as failure is not something that is commonly discussed. Some that I have interviewed told me they could not recall a failure, which is ridiculous and obviously nonsense. Observe how open and honest the candidate is when discussing the event. Can the person objectively identify the cause of failure? Did the person not own the failure and try to blame other team members? Or were they embarrassed to talk about it? The major objective of the question is to see how comfortable the candidate is at dealing with failure and whether they can analyze it postevent and see an opportunity to learn.

Constantly Learning

- Can you share an experience in which you had to learn a new skill at work within a short space of time?

1. What was the situation?
2. What was the skill required?

3. Why was the skill required?
4. How did you approach learning the skill?
5. How long did you take to learn it?
6. How did you apply the new skill?
7. What was the result?

This set of questions tests whether the candidate is willing to pick up new skills. Notice in their tone whether or not they are excited about the unknown. Was the candidate self-motivated or forced to learn? You can also get a better understanding of how resourceful they are. Did the person read a book, do research, reach out to experts, or talk to people inside or outside the company? How eager was the candidate to learn? How fast did they learn and apply their new knowledge? Was the candidate delighted to mention their new skill?

What Would Attract Potential Intrapreneurs?

You know that you want to hire intrapreneurs. But how do you make your company a compelling place to work for intrapreneurial talents? Here are the expectations intrapreneurs have with regard to organizations and teams.

Organization Level

- *A strong and innovative brand.* Branding says many things about a corporation. To attract intrapreneurs to join yours, your brand needs to portray a strong, innovative image so that candidates feel that you have a strong sense of mission such as bringing change or creating something new. People should feel proud to be recruited and, by joining, believe they are setting on a journey to bring a positive impact to the world.
- *A culture that promotes innovation.* The culture of the corporation should encourage people to innovate. Indeed, innovation should be in the DNA of the corporation and its employees. Refer to Chapter 5 for information on building a culture that nurtures intrapreneurship.

- *Publicly unknown innovation capabilities.* Talented people
  are looking for signs that you've developed your innovation
  capabilities over the years and will continue doing so into the
  future. Do you publicly market your innovation capabilities?
  Do you have innovation teams? Do you have a corporate
  venture arm? What new products have you launched recently?
  Have you filed any patents or developed unique technology
  in-house? These are all signs—things that potential recruits
  will look for to assess whether or not you walk the talk.
  Refer to Chapter 6 for more on the infrastructure required
  for cultivating intrapreneurship.

Team Level

Intrapreneurial talents look for factors that affect their daily work
life, such as working style and interaction with colleagues. They want
something very different from conventional work based on job security, a
reliable path to promotion, and a defined scope of work. Intrapreneurial
talents focus more on autonomy, flexibility, and growth opportunity.

- *Autonomy.* Intrapreneurs need room to exercise their creative
  muscles. Giving them autonomy empowers them to shape
  their working environment so that they can perform at their
  best. Working autonomously does not mean working in a silo
  or without guidance. It means that you put the employees
  in charge. It makes them feel valued and trusted. Autonomy
  usually comes from a direct manager who has a big influence
  on the work style of the team. As a leader, you should encourage people managers to build trust with their teams, delegate,
  and not micro-manage.
- *Flexibility.* There is an increasing demand for flexibility at
  work. More people now work across time zones, collaborating with people in different geographies. Telling an employee
  in Asia who needs late-night calls with a U.S. team to stick
  to nine o'clock to six o'clock office hours is unreasonable.
  During the pandemic, many people were required to work

from home or a hybrid of office and home. The freedom to choose when and where to work has grown into a priority for employees, balancing their roles at work with other aspects of life. Yet many corporations struggle to provide flexible working arrangements. Even though some have developed firmwide schemes, most employees are not aware of them or are reluctant to request flexible working. Having said that, the pandemic has definitely shaken conventional assumptions of people having to work from specific locations at particular times. A people-first approach should be taken when it comes to giving intrapreneurs the flexibility to approach how they want to get the job done.

- *Growth opportunity.* Intrapreneurs are eager to learn and advance. They also get bored with the status quo. The idea of having the opportunity to grow excites them. Growth does not necessarily mean promotion. It can include learning new skills, expanding their network, leading new projects, and making lateral moves. During the hiring process, leaders not only have to assess a candidate against the skills required for the role but also look at whether the role brings growth opportunities for the individual.

Intrapreneurship in Action: DBS Hack2Hire2

Some candidates are smart. They learn about the interview patterns of a company. During the one-hour conversation, the candidates can give you the model answers you want. Yet, when they get onboard, their actual performance might not live up to the expectation. Some companies realized that interviews only might not be the best hiring tool.

DBS, one of the largest banks in Southeast Asia, has determined to reimagine banking and the way it hires. To achieve that, it targets to hire the best technology talents who have a strong passion for new technologies and innovative individuals who want to drive major transformation. To ensure that the technology candidates it hires are as intrapreneurial and agile as they claim, DBS decided that the candidates should prove their capabilities via more hands-on tasks. Instead of interviews, DBS puts them through hackathons. During the hackathons, candidates are given specific problems or opportunities. They are paired with other candidates to explore and develop solutions. Through the hackathon, DBS would assess both the candidates' technical and problem-solving skills. Compared to interviews, a hackathon is more expensive as a hiring tool. However, the investment is worth spending as it ensures that the hired candidates can fulfill the expectation of the corporate.

Retain Intrapreneurs

Assuming you have hired the right intrapreneurial candidates, how do you keep them engaged and satisfied so that they contribute meaningfully to the corporation? Managing employee retention is difficult and managing intrapreneur retention is even harder. When intrapreneurial talents cannot find satisfaction in the workplace, other than joining another company, they might opt to become entrepreneurs themselves. That opens up many more options for intrapreneurs and makes it harder to retain them. Some intrapreneurs who are passionate about solving a problem become so attached to it that they would solve it outside (on their own or with another corporation) if they cannot innovate inside.

Feed Them Challenges

Intrapreneurs are motivated by challenges. They see challenges as opportunities to learn and have an impact. On the other hand, they are bored with routine. If the tasks they are assigned aren't challenging, they will quickly feel disengaged. So keep the intrapreneurs busy by giving them challenging tasks and problems to solve. They tend to move on to another challenge once one has been solved. Depending on the project duration, their mission needs to be refreshed from time to time. A new problem is a reset for them and keeps them motivated. It's good practice to open up your organization's book of problems for intrapreneurs to explore.

In Chapter 6, I discussed the use of idea management as a repository of ideas. Similarly, you can also craft a list of problem statements you want to innovate for and make it openly available to employees. Intrapreneurs can seek their next potential project to work on from the pool. The platform should enable intrapreneurs to access background material and reach out to the teams who are working on the problem.

Support the Growth of Intrapreneurs

Intrapreneurial talents need to learn about innovation methodology, project management, leadership, communications, and other skills to help them navigate a large organization. You should support them along their career journey. Corporate leaders and HR can partner to support the growth of intrapreneurs by:

- *Tailoring a personalized development plan.* Understand what skills the intrapreneurial talent does or doesn't have today, the skills they want to acquire, and how they can achieve their goals. Help them to identify suitable courses and materials and sponsor the training.
- *Providing mentorship.* Who in your organization today are seasoned intrapreneurs? Line them up to mentor potential intrapreneurs as role models. It is valuable for potential intrapreneurs to see and talk to someone who has been there and done it. The mentor should be able to share a large amount of organizational knowledge and best practice.
- *Creating an intrapreneurial career path.* Many people are afraid of building a career that's focused on problem solving. It would mean seeking solutions to various problems, potentially moving between different functions or fields regularly. However, intrapreneurs are excited by this. They are not afraid to venture outside of their comfort zone or original domain of expertise. However, this is a double-edged sword. The desire to explore the unknown causes them to move on from a particular domain in a relatively short time. It could be a couple of years or it could be a few months. This makes

it challenging for them to establish a solid career path. A conventional corporation usually requires people to progress within a vertical after achieving some level of seniority. Corporate leaders and HR need to understand that there is a new way of managing a career path. In fact, intrapreneurship by itself is a possible new career path. To help intrapreneurs advance their careers, organizations should support internal mobility, not just for lateral moves but also for promotions that aren't purely dictated by the amount of time spent in a particular department.

Reward Intrapreneurship

In Chapter 5, we have discussed how leaders can encourage intrapreneurship by offering rewards. In this section, we will focus more on corporate-level rewards that are not gestures or perks. They are policy-driven rewards built into the corporation's remuneration system. Some require big and bold decisions to be made. Depending on the corporate culture and its unique innovation ecosystem, corporate leaders and HR should consider carefully when to put these practices into place.

Reward With New Roles

If the idea involves building a new business, you should consider naming the intrapreneur team the C-suites of the new business when it is launched. Give the team the option to own and run the new business as entrepreneurs do. The new business is still under the umbrella of the corporation. The team members can become chief executive officer, chief financial officer, chief technology officer, chief operating officer, chief design officer, and so forth on the management team of the new business. The compensation should also match the new position to reflect what they are worth leading the new business.

Sometimes, not everyone on the intrapreneur team wants to take up a management position in a new business. It's normal for some to want to move on to other intrapreneurship projects. As a leader, what you can do is provide options and let the intrapreneur choose for themselves.

Intrapreneurship in Action: Citi D10XSM Program—Reward With New Roles[3]

Citi Ventures fostered intrapreneurship using an internal accelerator to support the creation, development, and launch of new concepts by employees. The program is designed to partner closely with core businesses to discover strategic growth areas to "propel Citi into the future." Over the years, it has inspired numerous intrapreneurs and launched many innovations, including Proxymity.

Dean Little and Jonathan Smalley worked at Citi in London and had over 30 years of combined experience in custody and asset-servicing product development. They identified a problem with the shareholding voting process of institutional clients.

Institutional clients owned shareholdings of hundreds or even thousands of other companies around the world. The clients couldn't attend all of those companies' shareholder meetings but they were required to vote during the meetings. Conventionally, agents and intermediaries collected voting agendas from the companies and notified all the investors. The investors then had to cast their votes and send them back to the agents and intermediaries. Depending on the complexity, there could be up to seven intermediaries involved. Unsurprisingly, misinterpretation and mistakes occurred. With so much time lost on simply communicating information, the time available for investor decision making was squeezed. The process was also very costly, with billions of dollars spent on it every year.

To solve the problem, Dean and Jonathan came up with an idea called Proxymity. It's an online platform that connects companies more directly with shareholders, removing most of the steps in between and the potential for errors. Meeting agendas and voting intentions are shared digitally. Proxymity helps companies to manage the process in real time, with less risk and more transparency.

During the discovery process, the team has felt that for Proxymity to have the largest possible impact, it should be backed by the industry as a whole. To support this vision, some of the world's largest financial institutions joined together to invest in the platform and establish

Proxymity as an independent business. As well as Citi, Proxymity is now backed by financial institutions including BNY Mellon, Deutsche Bank, HSBC, J.P. Morgan, and State Street.[4]

Dean and Jonathan have also crafted new careers. Dean became the CEO and Jonathan the COO of Proxymity. They are still partners and have been leading a team to further develop Proxymity as a new business.

Reward With Shareholdings

To motivate intrapreneurs to innovate for the company, they should be rewarded in a meaningful way. Granting employees a minority shareholding in the new business they build is one of the most powerful ways to motivate them to make the business successful. A good example of this is Henry Chesbrough, who in 1984 was an employee of Quantum Corporation, a hard drive manufacturer.[5] He was working in a team of four people that started Plus, a new business within Quantum. All of them were given shares in Plus, with Quantum taking 80 percent of the shareholding in return for funding the team. Each of them ended up earning quite a lot when Quantum bought back the remaining 20 percent of the stock in 1988, at a valuation of roughly $100 million.

Using shareholding as a reward provides the intrapreneur with a strong vested interest in the project they are building. They develop and operate the project as if it is their own business. In Henry's case, he chose to sell his shares back to Quantum. Employees might instead opt to keep their minority shareholding and right to dividends.

When you reward employees with shares, consider building in a vesting period to encourage long-term behavior. Awarding shares at an early stage, in only one allocation, might promote excessive risk-taking. A shareholding vesting mechanism could vest a portion of shares over several years or vest them based on performance.

Some corporations already have a corporate shareholding plan for employees. Based on employee performance, they are granted a small number of shares in the corporation (not the new business). Those incentives work quite well for senior management and, in general, all employees as they benefit from the overall growth of the company. However, motivating intrapreneurs using corporate shares might not work effectively as the linkage is weak. At an early stage, the revenue or cost-saving contribution of the innovation the intrapreneur is working on is too insignificant to influence the stock price of the corporate shares.

CHAPTER 10

What Could Kill Intrapreneurship?

In previous chapters, we discussed the components and setup of a corporate environment that cultivates and supports intrapreneurship. This chapter will cover the common pitfalls that can kill intrapreneurship. Pay attention to these signs, any one of which might become a roadblock in your organization.

Not Walking the Talk

Some corporations promote themselves as innovative and claim that they support intrapreneurs. They even make intrapreneurship a key priority in their strategy. But actions speak louder than words. What did the corporation invest in? What program did it set up? What practice has it put into place? What ideas did it support? Corporations need to demonstrate their commitment, or else innovation and intrapreneurship are just buzzwords to make a strategy look fancy. Messages to the outside world should be consistent with messages to employees. Employees feel confused when they read about innovation in the corporation's annual report and marketing campaign but do not see any activity in their workplace. Intrapreneurship shouldn't just be a catchy slogan. Find out which components you need to put in place to provide an ecosystem for intrapreneurship and sustainable innovation. Make a plan that is aligned with your corporate and innovation strategy and communicate it widely with your employees. Make the leadership team accountable for making those changes. Keep track of progress and share it transparently with your organization.

Unsupportive Middle Managers

In most cases, intrapreneurship requires top-down support, and C-suites are common early adopters as they see how this investment benefits their organization in the long run. Employees are also excited about intrapreneurship as they find a way to flex their creative muscles. They have ideas they cannot wait to pitch. But why do you not see more ideas coming from them? It could be because your middle management is an impediment. They might still be lukewarm toward the idea of intrapreneurship. They see it as a distraction from current productivity, shaking up their well-established routine. They are focused on their Key Performance Indicator (KPIs), which set targets they need to achieve in the near term. Any deviation from those affects their performance. What's in it for them to support an idea that might be realized in two years if they are measured against this year's targets. What's more, might their jobs be at risk if KPIs are not met? If their immediate supervisors and managers do not support intrapreneurship, employees will be skeptical about joining in, no matter how much top management wants to push it. At the end of the day, their supervisors have a direct influence on their performance evaluation, which affects their job security and rewards.

There are two ways to tackle this roadblock:

1. Build intrapreneurship or innovation metrics into your managers' KPIs. The major reason why middle managers are not aligned is that they are measured by conventional metrics which focus on the short-term goals of productivity and efficiency. Refer to the "Intrapreneurship Metrics" in Chapter 6. Find out which ones are relevant to your organization and build those into managers' metrics to encourage intrapreneurship activities in their business lines.
2. Build direct access to senior leaders. With limited access to top management, many good ideas can be buried or lost for various reasons. These include managers not seeing the value of the idea in their own business, the idea being deemed too big to execute in the department, or the idea seeming too futuristic. In this case, giving your employees direct access to pitch to top management or a panel is the recommended approach. Refer to the "Idea Evaluation Panel" in Chapter 6.

Groupthink

Have you heard someone say,

> The idea sounds good. Let's check with X in another department. We also need input from Y from this team. By the way, ask Z if this is in line with their plan too. I have no issue if they are all fine with it.

It is natural for people to seek input and alignment for an idea before they proceed. However, this process should neither take too long nor involve too many stakeholders. I have been in teams that have this groupthink culture. This cycle never ends, as once you check with the suggested person, that person then asks you to check with at least three more people to confirm. I have seen an intrapreneur having to seek input from more than 50 people over three months and still have no clue whether or not their idea can be pursued. After a while, the intrapreneur felt that they were going around in circles and became less passionate. Without a clear decision, they stopped pursuing their idea and walked away from it.

You should have a clearly defined process and roles to manage intrapreneurs' ideas and projects. The decision-making criteria and process should also be transparent to employees. Refer to "Idea Management" in Chapter 6 to find out more about how to set up a proper framework.

Intrapreneurial Theater

Many corporations that find themselves new to the intrapreneurship space, and lagging, naturally want to catch up in the game. The first thing they do is hire large consultancy firms to come up with strategies and plans. The consultants talk to the C-suite to find out the current state, advise them on all the best practices, build a playbook, and put together a blueprint. The next thing is innovation events. They host hackathons, bootcamps, and workshops. Every employee is excited to contribute and finds it fun to be involved. They feel energized and refreshed. The culture shifts. But nothing happens after the events. Why?

All of the activities up to this stage are intrapreneurial theater. The consultant work and events make people feel like intrapreneurship is important and they feel that the corporation is going to become more innovative. The activities were designed to help the employees "experience" innovation. Unfortunately, the events were not built around the objective of achieving sustainable innovation. Don't get me wrong: there is nothing wrong with the activities mentioned. It is the intention behind them. Corporate leaders need to recognize that intrapreneurial activity without a clear objective and infrastructure to support it is merely for show. Employees will feel inspired at that moment in time. But once they find out that the ideas from those activities are going nowhere, they will be more disappointed than ever. They will lose faith in your intrapreneurship talk. To avoid that, remember the following:

1. *Have a clear innovation-driven objective.* Target solving real problems and build new ideas that are aligned with your innovation strategy from innovation activities. The objective should never be the event itself.
2. *Provide infrastructure to progress.* Figure out the mechanism and support system before you launch the activity. Decide the framework for how the ideas can proceed and the resource that is put in place to support them. Don't leave ideas hanging or let the intrapreneurs figure them out for themselves.

Asking for Immediate ROI

Conventionally, estimated ROI is a typical metric that corporate leaders ask for before they decide whether or not to invest in a project. Some corporations set a minimum required return on their investment (e.g., 20 percent) and any project ROI should not be lower than that to justify the deployment of capital. Sometimes, due to the urgency of fulfilling business goals, the project team is expected to bring in the actual ROI within a short period. However, asking for immediate ROI endangers intrapreneurship.

First, the more disruptive the ideas are, the more uncertain the ROI is. For core and adjacent innovation, employees can still try to draw data from existing products or markets to estimate the ROI. But for disruptive ideas, there is no benchmark in the market. Because the product is brand new, it is challenging to estimate the pricing and profit in the early stage. Asking intrapreneurs for a solid estimated ROI is simply not realistic for disruptive ideas. By doing this, you will drive away disruptive ideas in the funnel, and only the core and adjacent ones will remain.

Second, many corporations require a product's launch to perform immediately to the ROI expected, and they shut down projects that are not up to ROI requirement. However, innovation is an iterative process and the first launch is usually an minimal viable product (MVP) to test the market for feedback. Based on the learnings, the team would pivot and adjust their offerings. If the corporation is asking for immediate ROI within the MVP launch period, it might risk losing a good idea by shutting it down too early.

Instead of asking for estimated ROI, evaluate the ideas using a more innovation-relevant framework. Allow the team to validate the idea using the proper innovation methodologies. Refer to "Idea Evaluation Framework" in Chapter 6. Embrace the uncertain nature of innovation and instead of asking for immediate ROI from each project, manage your innovation work as a portfolio. Some ideas will fail, some will break even, and some will provide your exponential growth. Refer to "Innovation Pipeline Management" in Chapter 6.

Bureaucratic Red Tape

Bureaucracy is the art of making the possible impossible.
—Javier Pascual Salcedo

Sociologist Max Weber defined bureaucracy as the systematic processes and organized hierarchies necessary to maintain order, maximize efficiency, and eliminate favoritism. Sounds nice, right? Unfortunately, I have never come across anyone in the workplace using the word "bureaucracy" as a positive word. Bureaucracy is usually associated with multiple layers, complex hierarchies, and complicated procedures and rules. Understandably, bureaucracy occurs in large organizations to maintain stability and reliable operations.

But the impact of bureaucratic red tape goes far beyond its intention. Rigid conformity to formal rules is considered redundant and hinders or prevents action or decision making. In their work "Emotional Responses to Bureaucratic Red Tape," Hattke, Hensel, and Kalucza found that bureaucratic red tape evokes significant negative emotional responses, especially confusion, frustration, and anger. The negative responses were evoked regardless of whether an individual perceives the bureaucratic procedure to be meaningful or meaningless.

In the study, they recognized that bureaucratic red tape creates delay and burden, which affects the individual's feeling about power and status, and this affects the person's emotions. They concluded that bureaucratic encounters are emotionally exhausting for individuals. Confusion, frustration, and anger may cause employees' inability to distinguish between functional rules and dysfunctional red tape.

Here's what your employees are feeling when they face different types of bureaucratic red tape:

- Intransparency: I have no idea about the situation/I do not know what is required of me/I do not know what it takes to get this done.
- Excessive rules and policies: Why is this necessary? What good does it do?
- Excessive approvals: I am not in a position to make any decision/I am not empowered/This is beyond my paid grade.
- Excessive procedures and paperwork: This is endless and whatever I do will take a long time/Things are slow/I am wasting my time.

Fighting bureaucratic red tape is one of the major reasons behind intrapreneur burnout. It is defined by feelings and behaviors such as loss of motivation, performance decrease, absenteeism, frequent resting or getting permission, and even walking off the job. This sort of behavior is clearly undesirable in any organization.[1]

In their work "Effect of the Burnout Syndrome on Intrapreneurship: A Practice in Province Ankara," Aykut Ekiyor and Gökçen Şenel studied the correlation between burnout and intrapreneurship.[2] In the study, they sampled employees working as nurses in Ankara X State Hospital. They found that burnout led to emotional exhaustion, depersonalization, and reduced personal accomplishment. The study further found that the results of burnout negatively impact intrapreneurial tendencies. Beware of what bureaucracy is costing your corporation.

To break down bureaucracy for intrapreneurship, you need to build both culture and infrastructure. Creating an ecosystem for intrapreneurship using the components discussed in Chapters 5 and 6 will help solve some of the issues caused by existing bureaucratic red tape.

Hiring Entrepreneurs Instead of Grooming Intrapreneurs

Many corporations recognize that they are weak in innovation. To rectify this, they seek entrepreneurial talent from the outside. They often look for serial entrepreneurs, people who are between entrepreneurial projects, or those who have built businesses before and want to rejoin the corporate world. They are hired because of their entrepreneurial experience.

Don't get me wrong. I am not saying that corporations should not hire entrepreneurs. In fact, there are many advantages that entrepreneurs can bring to the corporation. They might even be the best ones to question the status quo. However, it does not mean that the entrepreneurial job in your organization can only be done by external entrepreneurs. I have seen entrepreneurs get uncomfortable with corporate operations and struggle to navigate large organizations. Plus, hiring only outsiders to pick up innovative work sends the wrong message. It tells employees that they are not innovative enough and that their ideas do not matter.

Your employees deserve the chance to be at the forefront of innovation for your company as they know your customers, your product, and your strategy the best. Intrapreneurs should never be viewed as the second-best option for hiring entrepreneurs. There are pros and cons to both approaches. They are not mutually exclusive and, at times, entrepreneurs and intrapreneurs can complement each other's skillsets. As discussed in Chapter 7, the skills required of an intrapreneur are not entirely the same. In some areas, they even go beyond what is required of an entrepreneur.

I have discussed several practices in this chapter that can diminish your effort to build intrapreneurship. Take a moment to reflect on whether these scenarios occur in your organization today or would potentially be roadblocks when you kick-start your transformational journey. If so, research ways to tackle specific pitfalls using the tips mentioned under each section. Preempt the practices you need to put in place to ensure your investment is not wasted.

In the next and final chapter, we will discuss some actionable next steps and prepare you for building intrapreneurship in your organization.

CHAPTER 11

Intrapreneurship Boosters

From the previous chapter, you have read about things that can kill intrapreneurship, which you should avoid. How about what can help accelerate it? What if you are already building intrapreneurship based on the formula discussed but want something to boost it so you can achieve your goal even faster? This is the chapter for you. We will discuss boosters that help accelerate the execution of intrapreneurship, including the change of your employees' mindset, the speed of project execution, and the ROI you have made for intrapreneurship.

Remember, what we are going to talk about in this chapter are boosters, not the formula itself. To build a good and strong intrapreneurship foundation, you will need the factors of the formula to be in place. If you do not have a proper foundation, your employees will see through the tricks. Applying boosters without the formula would risk your employees' trust in your intrapreneurship initiatives in the long run. Always be mindful that the execution of boosters should be supported by the foundation of the formula.

Boosters for Mindset Change

Inspiration Series

If you are starting to build intrapreneurship, it is best to tap the experience of companies which have strong intrapreneurship practices. Have them come and share with your employees how they approach intrapreneurship. Ask them to share their success stories. These stories would become the inspiration for your employees. There are three types of companies that you can target to invite for sharing. Each represents a different perspective and potential takeaways:

1. Disruptor companies: These are the likes of technology-driven companies including Google and Amazon. These companies have started their development with strong intrapreneurship practices. They have pride in their culture nurturing innovation. They hire the best talents and offer the talents room to realize their ideas in the workplace. They formed the benchmark and best practices of intrapreneurship.
2. Conventional corporates which transformed: These are traditional corporates which were not strong at intrapreneurship before but have transformed over time. They have gone through the pain to successfully build intrapreneurship over time. They can share with you the reason why they decided to do it, the challenges involved, and the return they have achieved. They also set a good example to your corporate to encourage your employees that change might not come easy, but it is most certainly possible.
3. Startups in your field: You might find startups operating in a very different manner compared to your corporate. However, startups in your field might become your potential disruptor or allies. The way that startups work is usually highly customer-centric and agile. With innovative solutions, some startups can seize large market share over a short period. They also provide new perspectives of approaching a problem, potentially beyond the thinking of industry veterans. Since the startup is in your field, your employees can better relate to the problem they are trying to solve. The sharing from a startup also offers a great opportunity for a reality check as they could be potential competition.

Booster for Networking and Collaborations

1. Workspace redesign, physically and virtually
   Believe it or not, the design of the work environment does influence how people behave. In fact, a good designer knows that the purpose of a workplace design is to facilitate the desired work behavior. The traditional design of offices is surrounded by concepts of cubicles. It is highly purposed to keep the employees focused on their tasks

and away from distraction. The design was very much targeted at maximizing occupancy and increasing productivity. However, it is not primarily targeted at collaboration, creativity, or learning. Many companies including Meta (formerly known as Facebook), Airbnb, Google, and Amazon have come to realize that a traditional office design would not work if they wanted their employees to be innovative. Many have explored new designs below to encourage the natural collaboration and openness that is required for intrapreneurship.

a. Hot desks

The hot desk system frees employees from one definite seat assigned. Any employee can book any seat listed on the system in advance and work from there during the booked period. The employee should be given access to basic infrastructure including electricity, Wi-Fi connection, lockers, and so on. The arrangement of hot desks allows the employee to work in a different environment and meet colleagues who show up in the same hot desk location, who they might never meet otherwise. It encourages the employee to talk to people outside of their team or even departments to exchange notes about their work, get new perspectives, and learn about things outside of their domain. The growth of the network would help employees to get outside of their zone and explore thinking of other teams who are approaching different problems.

b. Modular desks

Modular desks are easy to move and can form different shapes to facilitate different working modes. They are like puzzles. The employees can pull the desk workshop and assemble the shapes they want them to be, be it the layout of individual workstations, small group meetings, workshops, or a theater. Modular desks provide the employees with flexibility, and they can determine how they like their spaces to be, depending on their needs.

Redesign of workspace is not for physical environment only. As remote working has become the new norm, many are relying on digital tools to get connected with their teams. Today, many employees are connected via digital tools and video conferencing. At first, the adoption of video conference tools like Google Meet, Zoom, and Microsoft Team brought much convenience to the organization. They allowed people to stay connected while working from home. However, many soon called out video conferencing fatigue and burnout. Some corporates have begun to set rules about video conferencing such as no back-to-back conferences or Zoom-free days. While soon we might see the end of a pandemic, it does not mean the end of remote working. Hybrid mode is expected for many in the future and some new roles are even designed entirely to be working remotely. So, what is the way to encourage natural virtual networking or collaboration?

c. Metaverse for virtual space

The concept of the metaverse is still relatively new, but worth paying attention to. While video conferencing is deemed old and boring, the metaverse is exciting and full of wonder. Experimenting with the metaverse workspace attracts the employees' curiosity. For most of the video conferencing tools, you only use them when you have a specific topic to meet with the team. No one keeps the video on and waits for people to come and chat. While video conferencing fulfills its purpose of being a meeting tool, it cannot be practically served as an effective networking tool. The metaverse, however, provides a potential solution to this problem. The metaverse provides a virtual space with an interesting design in which the employees can "hang out." They can design the look and outfit they show in the metaverse, build their own avatar, and interact with the others. When the technology is paired with the adoption of virtual and augmented reality, the metaverse can potentially offer a virtual space for teams to conduct whiteboarding, build prototypes, or even host social events.

Intrapreneurship in Action: The Accenture's Nth Floor[1,2]

To experiment with the metaverse office, Accenture has partnered with Microsoft and Altspace AR to launch the Nth floor, a virtual floor of Accenture where its employees can meet. The Nth floor brings a mixed reality experience for Accenture's employees to meet, hang out, and attend training together.

To enter the Nth floor, Accenture's employee creates an avatar, an individual character with a virtual body. Using that avatar and with a Virtual Reality (VR) device, the employee can immerse into the metaverse. The employees are present visually in a virtual space laid out just like an office. The Nth floor creates a more enriched experience than just a video conference. Using VR headsets and the virtual characters they created, the employees can move and look around their virtual office. They can also simulate presentation with gestures.

Office in the metaverse has yet been proven to be successful and it would take more time to become mainstream. However, it does prompt companies to rethink what virtual working means and how these alternatives can help them build better collaborations and their employee experience.

Boosters for New Ideas

The boosters in this section target situations when the number of ideas gathered from employees is falling behind expectations. To capture good or great ideas, you must first capture many ideas. However, you might be hearing employees saying that they have no clue about the customer problem, or they simply do not have a way of a solution. The employees are not the ones to blame. In fact, it is common that not all employees in a large corporate have direct touch with the customers. An employee sitting at the back office might not even know how exactly the customers use your products. The further away the employees are from the customers, the less they learn about the problems that need to be solved. Without these insights, it is challenging to inspire the employees to understand what customers are frustrated about or what their customers strongly desire. To solve this problem, bring your employees closer to your customers. Below are some quick ways you can help your employees learn more about your customers.

1. Customer problem repository

   In most corporates, customer insights are held in the hands of a small number of people. Mostly these are people who have direct access to customers, including sales and sometimes operations who handle complaints. Other employees who are not involved in customer servicing have a rare chance to gain access to these insights. Without these insights, let alone the right idea, they do not even know the right problem to solve.

   To create visibility, gather the key customer problem statements from various departments. Share these insights in a central repository with your employees. Make sure they know that these are the prioritized problems that the departments are trying to solve. While some problems are already being tackled by the respective departments, ideas are welcome. If the employees have ideas on how to solve those problems, connect them with the relevant department to contribute their ideas and perhaps take them further.

2. Design thinking bootcamp

   This is a step further from the above. If you already have a repository or list of problems that you want to solve, you can host a design thinking bootcamp. It is a series of activities designed to capture ideas within a timeframe, usually ranging from two to five days. During a design thinking bootcamp, employees are invited into an environment away from their usual business. They are brought into the bootcamp to team up and focus on the problem they were assigned. During the bootcamp, they would go through exercises designed to help them understand the problem, brainstorm for solutions, and gain validation within that timeframe. The problem assigned can be outside of their domain, but they will be provided the support of subject matter expertise. They would prototype the solution and at the end of the bootcamp, each team should have at least one solution concept with a low-fidelity prototype. The desired result of a design thinking bootcamp was less about having a solution built, but more about capturing ideas for future validation.

3. Customer-centric series

   This is more relevant to Business-to-Business (B2B) where your customers are corporates or small enterprises. Select some of your key customers. Remember to include both: those who demonstrate significant existing business and those who show potential growth in the future. Craft a series of content to allow your customers to provide insights into what is on their minds and the trends that they look out for. Have your customers share their thought leadership with your employees via talks, fireside chats, webinars, and so on. This would create space for your employees not just to focus on your business, but to better understand:

   • Your customers' current operating environment
   • Competition or disruption that your customers are facing

- Future trends that influence your customers and therefore
  your business as well

It allows your employees to expand their thinking beyond
their scope and tap into how they can help the customers grow
the business.

Boosters for Speedy Execution

Are you frustrated because you have heard enough ideas but not enough
progress? Do you find that there are more conversations than actual
execution? If you wonder how you can speed up the execution of the
ideas, consider the arrangements below:

1. Hackathons

   A hackathon is an event in which you can bring your teams together
   to focus on developing new solutions. It usually takes two to five
   days. Given the advancement of technology and the widely adopted
   agile practice, most new solution concepts can be developed into a
   working prototype within days. The structure of a hackathon can
   be similar to a design thinking bootcamp and therefore you might
   sometimes see elements of both being blended. The difference
   between the two is that the design thinking bootcamp focuses more
   on ideas, while the hackathon focuses more on development. It is
   therefore a natural extension of the design thinking bootcamp into
   the hackathon. During hackathons, project teams are paired with
   developers to solve a problem by developing a working prototype.
   This working prototype should prove the solution's technical feasibility, at least the key components of it. Because of its time-bound
   nature, the teams participating in hackathons are required to be
   highly focused and efficient.

   To further enhance the creativity of your employees, you may
   consider different types of hackathons:

   - Internal hackathon: Your employees are the only participants
     in the hackathon. The objective is to have your employees
     team up to solve problems for your corporate.

- Customer-partnered hackathon: Your hackathon is designed to solve the problems of your customers and your customers are open to cocreate with your teams. This is more common when your customers are corporates too. In this case, your teams will be assigned a customer problem and team up with customers or its representative(s) to develop the solution.
- Technology-partnered hackathon: Your hackathon is focused on helping your employees explore emerging or new technology. The purpose of the hackathon is to allow your employees to get comfortable with using these new tools so that they can explore more ideas in the future. For example, Microsoft sponsors corporate hackathons to help the corporate employee get used to Microsoft Power Apps, a low-code development platform that allows teams without coding skills to develop solutions.

2. Open innovation

Not all great innovation comes internally. It is becoming more common for corporates to experiment and practice open innovation. Open innovation provides the opportunity for corporates to tap on inspiration and resources beyond their own operating environment. Imagine if you can augment your intrapreneurs externally and have agile teams executing for the corporate without consuming more bandwidth of your teams. Most often, open innovation also results in a potential talent pipeline and partnerships that generate rewards in a long run.

Open innovation requires the corporate to share the problem or opportunities it is focusing on with an external audience. It is similar to a request for proposals. The external audience would submit ideas on how they propose to solve the problems. Moreover, the external audience will also be involved in building the solution together with the corporate.

Although the word "open" somehow suggests public context, the target audience of open innovation is often specific. Below are two common target audiences of open innovation:

- Academia: Corporates often partner with universities and academic research teams to explore emerging technologies or new solutions. In open innovation, the corporate shares its problem to be solved with universities and asks for team entries to pitch their ideas. A team with a successful pitch would be paired up with subject matter expertise to further the development of the solution. Depending on the nature of the problems, the corporate can target teams that specialize in relevant domains.

- Startups with commercialized products: For niche problems that require a quick solution rollout, corporates might prefer sourcing solutions that have a certain maturity. Open innovation allows the corporate to call for partnership with startups. The startups should have a relatively developed solution that the corporate can scale quickly. It is quite often that the solution developed needs customization or further development to fit the corporate's needs. Therefore, an intrapreneur is still required to sort out the design of the product leveraging the solution brought by the startup. Open innovation with startups provides advantages to the corporates as it offers speed and agility.

The idea of open innovation sounds quick and easy. However, do not underestimate the effort and time required to help the external team understand your business context and also the integration post-development. On top of those, be aware of the implication for your confidential data and intellectual property.

3. Intrapreneur hours

One of the most common problems that slow down the progress of an idea is the founder team's bandwidth. The founder team has their own duty to perform as they are hired to do so. Executing the idea becomes a second priority. They usually have to wait until all their primary job duties are completed, before they can work on the idea. Sometimes, it means that they are working extra hours for the idea. It might be fine within a short period. They are excited about the idea and driven by adrenaline. However, over time, their excitement would peak and begin to decline. They are buried by their work duties and stop progressing the idea. Give the intrapreneurs their "intrapreneur hours" to work on the idea. Make it a priority by providing them the required time to execute. For example, Google's "20% time" rule[3] gives its employees 20 percent of their time to work on ideas that interest them. That is equivalent to one day per workweek. Not all corporates can afford to offer that to all of their employees. What you can do is to offer this arrangement only to the founder teams with more maturity. The further they go through the funnel, the more time they can be assigned to work on the solution. It makes logical sense as the more matured the idea is, the higher chance it would become a new solution. The amount of work also increases as a new solution is to be developed and launched. When the founder team moves toward a proof-of-concept or pilot stage, consider allowing the team to dedicate more time to enhance their success rate.

CHAPTER 12

Setting Sail for Intrapreneurship

Now that you have finished reading this book and have the formula to build intrapreneurship in your organization, you are probably wondering, "Where do I start?" The Intrapreneurship Formula is a practical guide for leaders to understand the building blocks of intrapreneurship. I hope this book has stimulated your thought process, but I want it to do more. I hope it stimulates you to take action. Consider reading it to be merely the beginning of your journey, when you set up your organization for sustainable innovation by empowering your employees.

The pace of change has accelerated. Once, corporates were built to last for a century. Now, they might only last a decade. The pace of change is driven by the disruptive innovations brought about by the era of Industry 5.0. Today, how you empower your employees by building and managing intrapreneurship can make a difference to your business's survival and profitability in this rapidly changing environment.

You do not need to be the sole innovator for your business. Imagine that all your employees are proactively engaged in discovering new value. Their ideas could be the future drivers of your business. As a leader, your job is to be the corporate architect and craft an ecosystem that offers the components to help evaluate and develop those ideas. There's no doubt that the work required to build intrapreneurship is extensive but the return is worth the investment. It can open up new business opportunities and create competitive advantages that the management team might never have thought of.

Many leaders have found it challenging to build intrapreneurship because they think there is a lack of creative talent in their organization. The truth is that these talents simply haven't been identified. There are a list of traits of potential intrapreneurs mentioned in this book, which you can use to start identifying intrapreneurs in your workforce and begin training them. Some leaders may say that innovation activities seem chaotic and uncertain, and find it challenging to manage. But this is a misunderstanding common to those who have not found the Intrapreneurship Formula. It is, in fact, a disciplined process and needs to be complemented with a systematic approach. There are also clear metrics you can set to measure intrapreneurship.

Now I suggest you start by taking a moment to reflect. Do you recognize the challenges brought by Industry 5.0? Is your corporation under pressure to change? How do you manage intrapreneurship in your organization currently? Are your current practices set up for sustainable innovation? Are you committed to investing in empowering employees? Your honest answers matter. They will determine whether this book is mere weekend reading or will be the springboard for transforming your organization.

Next, engage your key leadership team. Give them this book and ask them to read it. Regroup with them to discuss the changing environment and the challenges brought by Industry 5.0. Ask them to share the disruption they have seen across industries, including the one in which your organization operates. Ask them to share their feelings about being told that one in two corporations will not maintain their leading position in the next 10 years. Help them understand that innovation is required for survival and that they will play a key role in creating the ecosystem.

Once you have senior leaders' buy-in, you should start to understand the existing state of intrapreneurship in your organization. You can do so by running the assessments in Chapter 2. Conduct Assessment I: Level of intrapreneurship in your corporate to discover existing assets, strengths, and areas of improvement. You should also engage your employees using Assessment II: The intrapreneur in you to discover your people's potential intrapreneurship traits and skills. Make an inventory of all the assessment results and form an action plan in partnership with your leadership team and HR. You can find the practical guide by referring to the relevant chapters in the book:

- Understand the traits of intrapreneurs to identify them in your employees (Chapter 3).
- Learn about components of the corporate ecosystem of innovation (Chapter 4).
- Create an intrapreneur-friendly culture (Chapter 5).
- Build the corporate infrastructure to cultivate intrapreneurship (Chapter 6).
- Understand the skills of successful intrapreneurs and provide this training to your employees (Chapter 7).
- Help your employees collaborate with intrapreneurs of different backgrounds (Chapter 8).
- Learn how to recruit and retain intrapreneurial talents (Chapter 9).
- Avoid the pitfalls that can kill intrapreneurship (Chapter 10).

You can find additional recommended resources at the end of the book. For tools, templates, further resources, and inquiries, visit the website at www.sandralam.me

Intrapreneurship of a large corporation seldom happens by accident. There are no happy coincidences of the kind sometimes enjoyed by start-ups. Intrapreneurship needs to be intentionally cultivated, nurtured, and constantly renewed. Top-down support and commitment from leaders play a significant role. Consider this book the starting point for transforming your organization.

Now is truly the best possible moment to take action. The next five to 10 years will see a big turnover in the ranks of leading corporates, providing exciting growth opportunities for outsiders that succeed at building sustainable innovation. The decisions you make today will determine the competitiveness, and even the survival, of your organization in decades to come. I hope you found this book helpful, and I wish you the best of luck as you drive your organization to success in the era of Industry 5.0.

Notes

Chapter 1

1. DXC Technology (2017).
2. Innosight, Anthony, Viguerie, and Waldeck (2016).
3. Chamorro-Premuzic (2020).
4. Schwab (2017).
5. Hermann, Pentek, and Otto (2016).
6. Olito (2020).
7. COVID Live—Coronavirus Statistics—Worldometer (n.d.).
8. BCG Executive Perspectives (2021).
9. Bar Am, Furstenthal, Jorge, and Roth (2020).
10. FAbramowitz (2017).
11. Viki (2020).

Chapter 2

1. McKinsey (2010).
2. McKinsey (n.d.).

Chapter 3

1. Chamorro-Premuzic (2014).
2. Dweck (2006).
3. Mace (2016).
4. Troy (2017).
5. Thirsty? Try On-The-Go H2O (n.d.).
6. Reindl (2019).
7. Borrelli (2019).
8. Portnoy (2017).

Chapter 4

1. Lewin (1936).
2. Lewin (2014).
3. Miller and Wedell-Wedellsborg (2013).

4. JBDAdmin (2019).
5. Emergenetics International (n.d.).
6. Infrastructure (n.d.).

Chapter 5

1. Edmondson (2018).
2. Detert and Edmondson (2007).
3. Gladwell (2011).
4. Amazon's global career site (n.d.).
5. Anders (2016).
6. Whittemore (2021).
7. Darmanin (n.d.).
8. Fiegerman (2013).
9. Dutt (2018).
10. Arsenault (2017).
11. Keswin (2017).
12. Starbucks (n.d.).
13. Starbucks (2016).
14. Clark (2020).
15. Brenner (2007a); Brenner (2007b).
16. Salesforce Research (2017).
17. DreamWorks Careers (n.d.); Bruzzese (2012).
18. Google for Work and Raconteur (2015).
19. Nielsen (2015).
20. Wong (2020).
21. Campbell (2017).
22. Edmondson (2014).
23. Cherry (2020a).
24. Pink (2011).
25. Warden (2016).
26. NASA People (n.d.).

Chapter 6

1. Martin (n.d.); Tsymbal (2021).
2. Güven (2020).
3. 3M's 15% Culture (n.d.).
4. Murphy (2020).
5. Scott (2012).

6. Yu and Malnight (2016).
7. BOXLAB Services GmbH (n.d.).
8. BOXLAB Services GmbH (n.d.).
9. Nagji and Tuff (2012a).
10. Nagji and Tuff (2012b).
11. Wiener-Bronner (2019).
12. Garcia (2019).
13. First Coke-Branded Energy Drink to Launch in the U.S. in 2020 (2019b).
14. Perch (2021).
15. About (n.d.).
16. Saltis (2020).
17. Coca-Cola (2021).
18. Coca-Cola and Wabi: revolutionary plan for local shops (2019).
19. Roush (2020).
20. Deloitte (2018).
21. What is the cloud? (n.d.).
22. What Is Cloud Computing? A Beginner's Guide (n.d.).
23. Pricing (n.d.).
24. Rojas (2019).
25. BBVA API_Market (2018).
26. 2020 State of the API Report | Brought to You by (n.d.).
27. Mitra (2015).
28. Koty (2020).
29. Sharkey (n.d.).
30. Dixon (n.d.).
31. Hunnam (2019).
32. Saran (2019).
33. Rossi (2019).
34. Govindarajan and Srinivas (2013).
35. Tansey (2018).
36. Trade secrets (n.d.).
37. Block, De Vries, Schumann, and Sandner (2014).
38. Fallon (2021).
39. IP ownership | IP Australia (2016).
40. Mirandah, Cubilla, Chandrasekaran, and Asia (2020).

Chapter 7

1. Introducing T-Shaped Managers: Knowledge Management's Next Generation (2001).
2. Akay (2015).

3. Cherry (2020a).

4. Design Kit (n.d.).

5. Kolawole (n.d.).

6. Ohno (1988).

7. Vredenburg (2017).

8. Ries (2011), p. 57.

9. Weisul (2020).

10. PillPack: Our story (n.d.)

11. Parker (n.d.).

12. Farr (2019).

13. What Is Kanban? An Overview of the Kanban Method (n.d.).

14. Mehrara (2021).

15. Grégoire (2020).

16. Forsythe, Kuhla, and Rice (2018).

17. COVID-19: Implications for business (2020).

18. How COVID-19 triggered the digital and e-commerce turning point | UNCTAD (2021).

19. Inam (2017).

20. Birkinshawa and Ridderstråleb (1999).

21. Schulte (2012).

22. Bruzzese (2012).

23. Flavell-While (2011); Bullen (2019).

Chapter 8

1. Erikson (2019).

2. Frome (2019).

3. Katila (2017).

Chapter 9

1. Sethi, Stubbings, Gratton, and Brown (2019).

2. DBS Hack2Hire Singapore 2022 (n.d.).

3. D10X—Internal Growth Model–Citi Ventures (n.d.).

4. Omenaka (2020).

5. Osterwalder (2015).

Chapter 10

1. Ekiyor and Şenel (2017a).
2. Ekiyor and Şenel (2017b), pp. 1–11.

Chapter 11

1. Pandey (2021).
2. Accenture Technology (2020).
3. Clark (2022).

References

2020 State of the API Report | Brought to You by. n.d. Postman. www.postman
.com/state-of-api/#key-findings (retrieved May 23, 2021).

3M's 15% Culture. n.d. *3M*. www.3m.co.uk/3M/en_GB/careers/culture/
15-percent-culture/ (retrieved May 24, 2021).

About. n.d. The Coca-Cola Company. https://investors.coca-colacompany
.com/about#:%7E:text=The%20Coca%2DCola%20Company%20
(NYSE,than%20200%20countries%20and%20territories (retrieved May 28,
2021).

Abramowitz, S. October 17, 2017. *Intrapreneurship Case Study of the Sony
Corporation's PlayStation by Intrapreneur Ken Kutaragi.* CEO Boardroom.
www.ceoboardroom.com/intrapreneurship-case-study-of-the-sony-
corporations-playstation-by-intrapreneur-ken-kutaragi/.

Accenture Technology. November 16, 2020. *Welcome to the Nth Floor—Accenture's
Virtual Office [Video].* YouTube. www.youtube.com/watch?v=lZttHYDgV64.

Akay, E. September 15, 2015. *Which Letter-shaped Will Future Employees and
Leaders Be?* LinkedIn.Com. www.linkedin.com/pulse/which-letter-shaped-
future-employees-leaders-esin-akay/.

Amazon's global career site. n.d. *Amazon Jobs.* www.amazon.jobs/en/principles
(retrieved June 04, 2021).

Anders, G. April 12, 2016. *Inside Amazon's Idea Machine: How Bezos Decodes
Customers.* Forbes. www.forbes.com/sites/georgeanders/2012/04/04/inside-
amazon/?sh=22b1e04f6199.

Arsenault, M. May 25, 2017. "How Valuable Is Amazon's 1-Click Patent? It's
Worth Billions." *Rejoiner.* https://rejoiner.com/resources/amazon-1clickpatent/.

Bar Am, J., L. Furstenthal, F. Jorge, and E. Roth. December 14, 2020. *Innovation
in a Crisis: Why It Is More Critical Than Ever.* McKinsey & Company. www
.mckinsey.com/business-functions/strategy-and-corporate-finance/our-
insights/innovation-in-a-crisis-why-it-is-more-critical-than-ever.

BBVA API_Market. September 17, 2018. *Brief History of APIs: From E-Commerce
to the Mobile Era.* www.bbvaapimarket.com/en/api-world/brief-history-apis-
e-commerce-mobile-era/

BCG Executive Perspectives. May 2021. *The Race for Innovation.* https://media-
publications.bcg.com/BCG-Executive-Perspectives-Race-for-Innovation.pdf.

Birkinshawa, J. and J. Ridderstråleb. 1999. *Fighting the Corporate Immune System: A Process Study of Subsidiary Initiatives in Multinational Corporations.* https://citeseerx.ist.psu.edu/viewdoc/download?doi=10.1.1.333.7562&rep=rep1&type=pdf.

Block, J., G. De Vries, J. Schumann, and P. Sandner. 2014. "Trademarks and Venture Capital Valuation." *Journal of Business Venturing* 29, no. 4, pp. 453–484.

Borrelli, C. July 05, 2019. *Who Created the McDonald's Happy Meal? 40 Years Later, the Answer Is Complicated.* Chicago Tribune. www.chicagotribune.com/entertainment/ct-ent-happy-meal-anniversary-0707-20190703-4c7xooiaubdlddo2qsbsuny3me-4c7xooiaubdlddo2qsbsuny3me-story.html

BOXLAB Services GmbH. n.d. *Chemovator.* www.chemovator.com/success-stories/boxlab-services-gmbh/ (retrieved February 26, 2022).

Brenner, R. March 21, 2007a. *Dismissive Gestures: I.* ChacoCanyon. https://chacocanyon.com/pointlookout/070321.shtml.

Brenner, R. March 28, 2007b. *Dismissive Gestures: II.* ChacoCanyon. https://chacocanyon.com/pointlookout/070328.shtml.

Bruzzese, A. July 19, 2012. *DreamWorks Is Believer in Every Employee's Innovation.* Houma Today. https://eu.houmatoday.com/article/DA/20120719/News/608082575/HC.

Bullen, E. September 12, 2019. *11 of the Best Brand Story Examples—Nicely Said.* Medium. https://medium.com/nicely-said/11-of-the-best-brand-story-examples-af098e4ea911.

Campbell, S. October 05, 2017. *10 Simple Ways to Build a Collaborative, Successful Work Environment.* Entrepreneur. www.entrepreneur.com/article/302126.

Chamorro-Premuzic, T. August 27, 2014. *Curiosity Is as Important as Intelligence.* Harvard Business Review. https://hbr.org/2014/08/curiosity-is-as-important-as-intelligence.

Chamorro-Premuzic, T. March 26, 2020. *Why You Should Become an "Intrapreneur."* Harvard Business Review. https://hbr.org/2020/03/why-you-should-become-an-intrapreneur (retrieved April 21, 2022).

Cherry, K. March 04, 2020a. *The Incentive Theory of Motivation Explains How Rewards Drive Actions.* Verywell Mind. www.verywellmind.com/the-incentive-theory-of-motivation-2795382.

Cherry, K. May 02, 2020b. *Why Empathy Is Important.* Verywell Mind. www.verywellmind.com/what-is-empathy-2795562.

Clark, D. January 07, 2022. *Google's "20% Rule" Shows Exactly How Much Time You Should Spend Learning New Skills—and Why It Works.* CNBC. www.cnbc.com/2021/12/16/google-20-percent-rule-shows-exactly-how-much-time-you-should-spend-learning-new-skills.html#:%7E:text=Enter%3A%20Google's%20%E2%80%9C20%25%20time,wrote%20in%20their%20IPO%20letter (retrieved February 27, 2022).

Clark, T.R. 2020. *The 4 Stages of Psychological Safety: Defining the Path to Inclusion and Innovation* [E-book]. Berrett-Koehler Publishers. www.amazon.sg/Stages-Psychological-Safety-Inclusion-Innovation/dp/1690586095.

Coca-Cola and Wabi: revolutionary plan for local shops. December 05, 2019. iProUP. www.iproup.com/economia-digital/9590-coca-cola-and-wabi-revolutionary-plan-for-local-shops#:%7E:text=In%20this%20context%2C%20Coca%2DCola,join%20the%20digital%20revolution.Strategy.

Coca-Cola. 2021. *The Coca-Cola Company 2020 Business & Environmental, Social and Governance Report.* https://d1io3yog0oux5.cloudfront.net/cocacolacompany/files/pages/cocacolacompany/db/761/description/coca-cola-business-environmental-social-governance-report-2020.pdf.

COVID Live—Coronavirus Statistics—Worldometer. n.d. *Worldometer.* www.worldometers.info/coronavirus/ (retrieved March 12, 2022).

COVID-19: Implications for business. June 25, 2020. *COVID-19: Briefing note #11: June 25, 2020.* McKinsey & Company. www.mckinsey.com/business-functions/risk/our-insights/covid-19-implications-for-business.

D10X—Internal Growth Model—Citi Ventures. n.d. Citi Ventures. www.citi.com/ventures/d10x.html (retrieved May 23, 2021).

Darmanin, D. n.d. *Core Company Values: 100 Examples & How We Built Ours.* Hotjar. www.hotjar.com/blog/company-values/#:%7E:text=Company%20values%20(also%20called%20corporate,customer%20relationships%2C%20and%20company%20growth (retrieved June 04, 2021).

DBS Hack2Hire Singapore. 2022. DBS.Com. www.dbs.com/hack2hire/sg/index.html (retrieved February 27, 2022).

Deloitte. June 14, 2018. "How Cloud Can Boost Innovation." *CIO Journal—WSJ.* https://deloitte.wsj.com/cio/2018/06/15/how-cloud-can-boost-innovation-2/.

Design Kit. n.d. *Design Kit.* www.designkit.org/ (retrieved May 13, 2021).

Detert, and Edmondson. 2007. *Why Employees Are Afraid to Speak.* Harvard Business Review. https://hbr.org/2007/05/why-employees-are-afraid-to-speak.

Dixon, M. n.d. *How Netflix Used Big Data and Analytics to Generate Billions.* Selerity. https://seleritysas.com/blog/2019/04/05/how-netflix-used-big-data-and-analytics-to-generate-billions/#:%7E:text=Netflix%20collects%20several%20data%20points,data%20to%20a%20TV%20show (retrieved May 26, 2021).

DreamWorks Careers. n.d. *DreamWorks.* www.dreamworks.com/careers (retrieved May 23, 2021).

Dutt, A. August 31, 2018. "Tech in Asia—Connecting Asia's Startup Ecosystem." *Tech in Asia.* www.techinasia.com/amazons-oneclick-purchase-feature-order-changed-game.

Dweck, C. 2006. *Mindset: The New Psychology of Success.* Random House.

DXC Technology. July 19, 2017. *Digital Transformation Is Racing Ahead and No Industry Is Immune.* Harvard Business Review. https://hbr.org/sponsored/2017/07/digital-transformation-is-racing-ahead-and-no-industry-is-immune-2.

Edmondson, A. August 01, 2014. *Strategies for Learning From Failure.* Harvard Business Review. https://hbr.org/2011/04/strategies-for-learning-from-failure.

Edmondson, A.C. 2018. *The Fearless Organization: Creating Psychological Safety in the Workplace for Learning, Innovation, and Growth* (1st ed.). Wiley.

Ekiyor, A. and G. Şenel. June 2017a. "Effect of the Burnout Syndrome on Intrapreneurship: A Practice in Province Ankara." *Asian Journal of Economics, Business and Accounting.* www.journalajeba.com/index.php/AJEBA/article/download/9986/17871/.

Ekiyor, A. and G. Şenel. 2017b. "Effect of the Burnout Syndrome on Intrapreneurship: A Practice in Province Ankara." *Asian Journal of Economics, Business and Accounting* 3, no. 2, pp. 1–11. https://doi.org/10.9734/ajeba/2017/33946.

Emergenetics International. n.d. "What Is Corporate Culture and How It Affects Performance." *Emergenetics.* https://emergenetics.com/blog/corporate-culture-affect-performance/ (retrieved June 04, 2021).

Erikson, T. 2019. *Surrounded by Idiots: The Four Types of Human behavior (or, How to Understand Those Who Cannot Be Understood).*

Fallon, N. May 14, 2021. *Can an Employee Own Intellectual Property?* US Chamber of Commerce. www.uschamber.com/co/start/strategy/can-employees-own-intellectual-property.

Farr, C. 2019. *The Inside Story of Why Amazon Bought PillPack in Its Effort to Crack the $500 Billion Prescription Market.* www.cnbc.com/2019/05/10/why-amazon-bought-pillpack-for-753-million-and-what-happens-next.html.

Fiegerman, S. December 13, 2013. *Netflix's Data Points Are Not the Usual Suspects.* Mashable. https://mashable.com/2013/12/11/netflix-data/?europe=true#xyc3NyJWdaqO.

First Coke-Branded Energy Drink to Launch in the U.S. in 2020. October 01, 2019b. The Coca-Cola Company. www.coca-colacompany.com/news/coke-energy-drink-launches-in-2020.

Flavell-While, C. May 2011. *Victor Mills–A "Pampered" Career.* Features—The Chemical Engineer. www.thechemicalengineer.com/features/cewctw-victor-mills-a-pampered-career/.

Forsythe, G., K. Kuhla, and D. Rice. August 08, 2018. *Understanding the Challenges of a VUCA Environment.* ChiefExecutive.Net. https://chiefexecutive.net/understanding-vuca-environment/.

Frome, N. 2019. *This Is the Perfect Team Size for Innovation According to 300+ Decision-Makers.* https://medium.com/agileinsider/this-is-the-perfect-team-size-for-innovation-according-to-300-decision-makers-a0a6eed

745a0#:~:text=Rather%2C%20almost%20nine%20in%20ten,teams%20 when%20making%20important%20decisions.

Garcia, T. April 24, 2019. *Coca-Cola Gets a Boost From Coke Zero Sugar, Coke Orange Vanilla and Mini Cans*. MarketWatch. www.marketwatch.com/story/ coca-cola-gets-a-boost-from-coke-zero-sugar-coke-orange-vanilla-and-mini-cans-2019-04-23.

Gladwell, M. 2011. *Outliers: The Story of Success* (1st ed.). Back Bay Books.

Google for Work & Raconteur. January 2015. *Working Better Together: A Study of Collaboration and Innovation in the Workplace*. https://storage.googleapis .com/gfw-touched-accounts-pdfs/Collaboration%20Study%20-%20 June%202015.pdf.

Govindarajan, V. and S. Srinivas. August 06, 2013. *The Innovation Mindset in Action: 3M Corporation*. Harvard Business Review. https://hbr.org/2013/08/ the-innovation-mindset-in-acti-3#:%7E:text=3M%20has%20several%20 mechanisms%20to,successful%20achievement%20of%20this%20goal.

Grégoire, P. February 28, 2020. *Stakeholder Mapping: Identify & Assess Project Stakeholders*. Boréalis. www.boreal-is.com/blog/stakeholder-mapping-identify-stakeholders/.

Güven, B. January 2020. "The Integration of Strategic Management and Intrapreneurship: Strategic Intrapreneurship From Theory to Practice." *Business and Economics Research Journal*. https://doi.org/10.20409/berj.2020.247.

Hermann, M., T. Pentek, and B. Otto. January 05, 2016. *Design Principles for Industrie 4.0 Scenarios*. IEEE Conference Publication | IEEE Xplore. https:// ieeexplore.ieee.org/document/7427673/?arnumber=7427673&newsearch= true&queryText=industrie%204.0%20design%20principles.

How COVID-19 triggered the digital and e-commerce turning point | UNCTAD. March 15, 2021. UNCTAD. https://unctad.org/news/how-covid-19-triggered-digital-and-e-commerce-turning-point.

Hunnam, O. May 23, 2019. "Real Life Examples of True Data Driven Innovation." *Idea Drop | Idea Management Software*. https://ideadrop.co/ customer-success/examples-of-data-driven-innovation/.

Inam, H. October 19, 2017. *To Lead In A VUCA World, Practice Leadership Agility*. Forbes. www.forbes.com/sites/hennainam/2017/10/18/to-lead-in-a-vuca-world-practice-leadership-agility/?sh=4fe0e8522190.

Infrastructure. n.d. *In Cambridge Dictionary*. https://dictionary.cambridge.org/ dictionary/english/infrastructure (retrieved April 28, 2021).

Innosight, S. Anthony, S. Viguerie, and A. Waldeck. 2016. *Corporate Longevity: Turbulence Ahead for Large Organizations*. Innosight. www.innosight.com/ wp-content/uploads/2016/08/Corporate-Longevity-2016-Final.pdf.

Introducing T-Shaped Managers: Knowledge Management's Next Generation. March 2001. Harvard Business Review. https://hbr.org/2001/03/introducing-t-shaped-managers-knowledge-managements-next-generation.

IP ownership | IP Australia. March 21, 2016. IP Australia. www.ipaustralia.gov
.au/understanding-ip/getting-started-ip/ip-ownership.

JBDAdmin, A. May 25, 2019. *Principles of Good Architecture.* IDesignWiki
. www.idesign.wiki/tag/principles-of-good-architecture/.

Katila, R. 2017. *Too Many Experts Can Hurt Your Innovation Projects.* https://hbr
.org/2017/12/too-many-experts-can-hurt-your-innovation-projects.

Keswin, E. November 16, 2017. *Use Stories From Customers to Highlight Your
Company's Purpose.* Harvard Business Review. https://hbr.org/2017/06/use-
stories-from-customers-to-highlight-your-companys-purpose.

Kolawole, E. n.d. *Design Kit.* www.designkit.org/mindsets/4 (retrieved May 13,
2021).

Koty, R. April 08, 2020. *APIs: The Foundation for Innovation.* Interconnections—The
Equinix Blog. https://blog.equinix.com/blog/2020/04/08/apis-the-foundation-
for-innovation/#:%7E:text=APIs%20allow%20companies%2C%20their%20
partners,pathways%20for%20innovation%20and%20growth.&text=are%20
making%20APIs%20available%20to,new%20solutions%20for%20their
%20customers.

Lewin, K. 1936. *Principles of Topological Psychology.*

Lewin, K. 2014. *A Dynamic Theory of Personality—Selected Papers,* pp. 115–116.
Lewin Press.

Mace, M. September 23, 2016. *On-the-Go H2O Spearheads Ford's Company-
Wide Innovation Drive at "Record Pace."* Edie.Net. www.edie.net/news/8/
On-the-go-H2O-spearheads-Ford-s-company-wide-innovation-drive-at—
record-pace-/.

Martin, G. n.d. *Top 10 Emerging Trends in Health Care for 2021: The New
Normal | AHA.* AHA Trustee Services. https://trustees.aha.org/top-10-
emerging-trends-health-care-2021-new-normal (retrieved May 21, 2021).

McKinsey. August 01, 2010. *Innovation and commercialization, 2010: McKinsey
Global Survey results.* McKinsey & Company. www.mckinsey.com/business-
functions/strategy-and-corporate-finance/our-insights/innovation-and-
commercialization-2010-mckinsey-global-survey-results#:%7E:text=As%20
companies%20begin%20to%20refocus,recent%20McKinsey%20Global%20
Survey%2C1&text=84%20percent%20of%20executives%20say,to
%20their%20companies'%20growth%20strategy.

Mckinsey. n.d. *Growth & Innovation | Strategy & Corporate Finance.* McKinsey
& Company. www.mckinsey.com/business-functions/strategy-and-corporate-
finance/how-we-help-clients/growth-and-innovation (retrieved June 29, 2021).

Mehrara, M. December 15, 2021. *Zooming Towards Human Connection—The
Airbnb Tech Blog.* Medium. https://medium.com/airbnb-engineering/zooming-
towards-human-connection-66bb6e45161c (retrieved Fevruary 17, 2022).

Miller, P. and T. Wedell-Wedellsborg. 2013. *Innovation as Usual: How to Help Your People Bring Great Ideas to Life*. Harvard Business Review Press.

Mind Tools Content Team. n.d. *5 Whys: Getting to the Root of a Problem Quickly*. Mind Tools. www.mindtools.com/pages/article/newTMC_5W.htm (retrieved June 04, 2021).

Mirandah, G., J. Cubilla, P. Chandrasekaran, and M. Asia. December 01, 2020. "Thomson Reuters Portal (Beta) Signon." *Thomson Reuters Practical Law*. https://content.next.westlaw.com/Document/I86715e10397611e798dc8 b09b4f043e0/View/FullText.html?contextData=(sc.Default)& transitionType=Default&firstPage=true.

Mitra, R. April 09, 2015. *API Strategy 201: Private APIs vs. Open APIs*. API Academy. https://apiacademy.co/2015/04/api-strategy-201-private-apis-vs-open-apis/.

Murphy, B. November 11, 2020. *Google Says It Still Uses the "20-Percent Rule," and You Should Totally Copy It*. Inc.Com. www.inc.com/bill-murphy-jr/ google-says-it-still-uses-20-percent-rule-you-should-totally-copy-it.html.

Nagji, B. and G. Tuff. May 2012a. *Managing Your Innovation Portfolio*. Harvard Business Review. https://hbr.org/2012/05/managing-your-innovation-portfolio.

Nagji, B. and G. Tuff. May 2012b. *Managing Your Innovation Portfolio*. Harvard Business Review. https://hbr.org/2012/05/managing-your-innovation-portfolio.

NASAPeople. n.d. *NASAPeople*. https://nasapeople.nasa.gov/awards/award_ criteria.htm (retrieved June 04, 2021).

Nielsen. March 2015. *How Collaboration Drives Innovation Success*. www .nielsen.com/wp-content/uploads/sites/3/2019/04/how-collaboration-drives-innovation-success-march-2015-1.pdf.

Ohno, T. 1988. *Toyota Production System: Beyond Large-Scale Production*. Portland, OR: Productivity Press. ISBN 0-915299-14-3.

Olito, F. August 21, 2020. *The Rise and Fall of Blockbuster*. Business Insider Nederland. www.businessinsider.nl/rise-and-fall-of-blockbuster?international =true&r=US.

Omenaka, K. July 31, 2020. *Proximity*. Proxymity. https://proxymity.io/.

Osterwalder, A. August 06, 2015. *Why Intrapreneurs Are Not Rewarded Like Sales People and Why This Needs To Change*. Strategyzer. www.strategyzer.com/blog/ posts/2015/8/6/why-intrapreneurs-are-not-rewarded-like-sales-people.

Pandey, K. December 29, 2021. *Virtual Office in The Metaverse—The Accenture Nth Floor*. Jumpstart Magazine. www.jumpstartmag.com/virtual-office-in-the-metaverse-the-accenture-nth-floor/ (retrieved February 27, 2022).

Parker, T.J. n.d. *Part 2: How Minimal Can My MVP Be*. www.pillar.vc/playlist/ audio/how-minimal-can-my-mvp-be/.

Perch, D. April 16, 2021. *Coca-Cola Target Market Analysis*. The Social Grabber. https://thesocialgrabber.com/coca-cola-target-market/.

Pink, D.H. 2011. *Drive: The Surprising Truth About What Motivates Us*. Riverhead Books.

Portnoy, E. January 02, 2017. *McDonald's Sells Over 250 Happy Meals Every Three Seconds*. Sense360 By Medallia. https://sense360.com/2016/08/30/mcdonalds-sells-over-250-happy-meals-every-three-seconds/.

Pricing. n.d. *Amazon Web Services, Inc.* https://aws.amazon.com/pricing/?pg=WIAWS-N&tile=learn_more (retrieved May 23, 2021).

Reindl, A. September 18, 2019. *The McDonalds Happy Meal Was Invented By a Latina and Here's How It Got Started*. MITÚ. https://wearemitu.com/wearemitu/entertainment/did-you-know-the-first-happy-meal-was-invented-by-a-latina/.

Ries E. 2011. *The Lean Startup: How Today's Entrepreneurs Use Continuous Innovation to Create Radically Successful Businesses*, p. 57.

Rojas, N. September 30, 2019. *Business Benefits of Sandbox Environment*. Digital Doughnut. www.digitaldoughnut.com/articles/2019/september/business-benefits-of-sandbox-environment.

Rossi, B. July 09, 2019. *Empowering Employees to Think Like Data Scientists*. Raconteur. www.raconteur.net/empowering-employees-to-think-like-data-scientists/.

Roush, J. May 13, 2020. *IT Infrastructure & Components: An Introduction*. BMC Blogs. www.bmc.com/blogs/what-is-it-infrastructure-and-what-are-its-components/.

Salesforce Research. January 2017. *The Impact of Equality and Values Driven Business*. www.salesforce.com/content/dam/web/en_us/www/assets/pdf/datasheets/salesforce-research-2017-workplace-equality-and-values-report.pdf.

Saltis, S. December 16, 2020. *D2C Benefits: Here's Why Manufacturers Are Going D2C*. Core Dna. www.coredna.com/blogs/direct-to-consumer-benefits#:%7E:text=D2C%20%5Ballows%20manufacturers%5D%20to%20make,it's%20a%20total%20win%2Dwin.&text=This%20new%20way%20of%20distribution,%2C%20CEO%2C%20CNC%20Machines%20Network.

Saran, C. October 21, 2019. *Many Companies Fail to Empower Employee Data-Driven Decision-Making*. ComputerWeekly.Com. www.computerweekly.com/news/252472588/Many-companies-fail-to-empower-employee-data-driven-decision-making.

Schulte, E. October 31, 2012. *The Intrapreneur's Playbook*. Fast Company. www.fastcompany.com/3002459/intrapreneurs-playbook.

Schwab, K. 2017. *The Fourth Industrial Revolution* (Illustrated ed.). Crown.

Scott, K. December 07, 2012. *The LinkedIn [in]cubator*. LinkedIn. https://blog.linkedin.com/2012/12/07/linkedin-incubator#:%7E:text=Once%20a%20quarter%2C%20any%20LinkedIn,turning%20their%20ideas%20into%20reality.

Sethi, B., C. Stubbings, L. Gratton, and J. Brown. 2019. *Secure Your Future People Experience.* PwC. www.pwc.com/gx/en/people-organisation/pdf/secure-your-future-people-experience-pwc.pdf.

Sharkey, M. n.d. *What Are APIs and How Can They Help Turn Your Company Into a Community?* Workplace from Facebook. www.workplace.com/blog/using-api-to-build-communities-at-work (retrieved May 26, 2021).

Starbucks. February 16, 2016. *Starbucks Stories and News.* https://stories.starbucks.com/stories/2016/starbucks-barista-learns-sign-language-for-a-customer/.

Starbucks. n.d. *Starbucks Stories and News.* https://stories.starbucks.com/ (retrieved June 04, 2021).

Tansey, C. June 07, 2018. *The Role of IP in Innovation.* Shelston IP. https://shelstonip .com/insights/publications/the-role-of-ip-in-innovation/#:%7E:text= Intellectual%20property%20(IP)%2C%20and,barriers%20to%20entry%20 for%20competition.

Thirsty? Try On-The-Go H2O. n.d. *Ford.* https://corporate.ford.com/articles/ sustainability/thirsty-try-on-the-go-h2o.html (retrieved June 04, 2021).

Trade secrets. n.d. *World Intellectual Property organization.* www.wipo.int/ tradesecrets/en/ (retrieved May 23, 2021).

Troy, T. April 02, 2017. "Ford's "On-the-Go H2O" Is a finalist in World Changing Ideas Awards." Cleveland. www.cleveland.com/automotive/plaindealer/2017/ 04/fords_on-the-go_h2o_is_a_finalist_in_world_changing_ideas_awards.html.

Tsymbal, O. April 28, 2021. *Technology Trends in Healthcare in 2021: The Rise of AI.* MobiDev. https://mobidev.biz/blog/technology-trends-healthcare-digital-transformation.

Viki, T. June 29, 2020. *Why Intrapreneurs Are Not Just Entrepreneurs Working Inside Large Companies.* Forbes. www.forbes.com/sites/tendayiviki/2020/06/28/ why-intrapreneurs-are-not-just-entrepreneurs-working-inside-large-companies/?sh=52d6f7e3483a.

Vredenburg, K. December 06, 2017. *Pivoting IBM Into a Design-led Intrapreneurial Enterprise—Karel Vredenburg (IBM).* Innov8rs. https://innov8rs.co/past-events/toronto-17/pivoting-ibm-design-led-intrapreneurial-enterprise-karel-vredenburg-ibm/.

Warden, T. 2016. *The Role of Rewards in Creating a Culture of Innovation.* Korn Ferry Focus. https://focus.kornferry.com/reward-and-benefits/the-role-of-rewards-in-creating-a-culture-of-innovation/.

Weisul, K. February 06, 2020. *How This Startup Is Taking the Frustration Out of Multiple Medications.* Inc.Com. www.inc.com/kimberly-weisul/2016-30-under-30-pillpack.html.

What Is Cloud Computing? A Beginner's Guide. n.d. Microsoft Azure. https://azure.microsoft.com/en-us/overview/what-is-cloud-computing/ (retrieved May 26, 2021).

What Is Kanban? An Overview of the Kanban Method. n.d. Digite. www.digite .com/kanban/what-is-kanban/#:%7E:text=It%20all%20started%20in%20 the,every%20stage%20of%20production%20optimally (retrieved June 04, 2021).

What is the cloud? n.d. Cloudflare. www.cloudflare.com/learning/cloud/what-is-the-cloud/ (retrieved May 23, 2021).

Whittemore, C.B. April 12, 2021. "What Great Brands Do With Mission Statements: 27 Examples." *Simple Marketing Now*. www.simplemarketingnow .com/blog/flooring-the-consumer/bid/168520/what-great-brands-do-with-mission-statements-8-examples.

Wiener-Bronner, D. February 08, 2019. *Coke Launches New Flavor to Bring in Customers*. CNN. https://edition.cnn.com/2019/02/08/business/coca-cola-new-flavor/index.html.

Wong, L. December 22, 2020. *11 Ways to Improve Collaboration Between Departments*. Workzone. www.workzone.com/blog/9-ways-to-improve-collaboration-between-departments/.

www.dlapiperintelligence.com/goingglobal/intellectual-property/index.html? t=employment-context&c=AU&s=employees.

www.pillpack.com/press#:~:text=Our%20Story,was%20built%20to%20fix%20 pharmacy.&text=After%20making%20it%20their%20mission,five%20 prescription%20medications%20a%20day.

Yu, H., and T. Malnight. July 14, 2016. *The Best Companies Aren't Afraid to Replace Their Most Profitable Products*. Harvard Business Review. https:// hbr.org/2016/07/the-best-companies-arent-afraid-to-replace-their-most-profitable-products.

Recommended Reading
and Courses

Recommended Reading

Knapp, J. 2016. *Sprint: How to Solve Big Problems and Test New Ideas in Just Five Days.*

Lewrick, M., J. Thommen, and L. Leifer. 2020. *The Design Thinking Life Playbook: Empower Yourself, Embrace Change, and Visualize a Joyful Life* (1st ed.). Wiley.

Liedtka, J., A. King, and K. Bennett. 2013. *Solving Problems With Design Thinking: Ten Stories of What Works* (Columbia Business School Publishing) (Illustrated ed.). Columbia Business School Publishing.

Ries, E. 2011. *The Lean Startup: How Constant Innovation Creates Radically Successful Businesses.*

Recommended Courses

- Foundations in design thinking certificate by IDEO U
- Design thinking bootcamp by Stanford d.school
- Mastering design thinking by MIT Management Executive Education
- Scrum: The basic by LinkedIn Learning
- Agile project management by edX
- Managing an agile team by Coursera

About the Author

Sandra Lam is a corporate innovation practitioner. She was the Senior Vice President, Innovation Catalyst, and Partnerships Lead at Citi Innovation Lab, a team within Citi which specializes in new product development, intrapreneurship, and external partnerships.

Sandra has more than 15 years of experience in the field of corporate innovation and the financial industry. She is a frequent keynote speaker at global innovation and FinTech forums. She has worked with leaders and managers globally to deliver innovative solutions. She has launched and managed intrapreneurship programs in large corporations to transform employees into founders. She has also led open innovation with outreach of more than thousands of FinTechs globally.

Sandra holds a Sloan Fellows MBA degree from Massachusetts Institute of Technology. She also holds a master's degree of IT in business from Singapore Management University and a Bachelor of Business Administration from the University of Hong Kong. Her background across business and technology has enabled her to navigate technological advancement in a dynamic and ever-changing business landscape.

Connect with Sandra on LinkedIn www.linkedin.com/in/sandralamyayui/

For more resources related to this book, visit www.sandralam.me

Index

OTHER TITLES IN THE HUMAN RESOURCE MANAGEMENT AND ORGANIZATIONAL BEHAVIOR COLLECTION

Michael Provitera, Barry University, Editor

- *Innovation Soup* by Sanjay Puligadda and Don Waisanen
- *Change Fatigue Revisited* by Richard Dool and Tahsin I. Alam
- *Versatility in the Age of Specialization* by Angela Cotellessa
- *Championing the Cause of Leadership* by Ted Meyer
- *Embracing Ambiguity* by Michael Edmondson
- *Breaking the Proactive Paradox* by Tim Baker
- *The Modern Trusted Advisor* by MacKay Nancy and Weiss Alan
- *Achieving Success as a 21st Century Manager* by Dean E. Frost
- *A.I. and Remote Working* by Miller Tony
- *Best Boss!* by Ferguson Duncan, Toni M. Pristo, and John Furcon
- *Managing for Accountability* by Curry Lynne
- *Fundamentals of Level Three Leadership* by Clawson James G.S.
- *Emotional Connection: The EmC Strategy* by Gershfeld Lola and Sedehi Ramin

Concise and Applied Business Books

The Collection listed above is one of 30 business subject collections that Business Expert Press has grown to make BEP a premiere publisher of print and digital books. Our concise and applied books are for...

- Professionals and Practitioners
- Faculty who adopt our books for courses
- Librarians who know that BEP's Digital Libraries are a unique way to offer students ebooks to download, not restricted with any digital rights management
- Executive Training Course Leaders
- Business Seminar Organizers

Business Expert Press books are for anyone who needs to dig deeper on business ideas, goals, and solutions to everyday problems. Whether one print book, one ebook, or buying a digital library of 110 ebooks, we remain the affordable and smart way to be business smart. For more information, please visit www.businessexpertpress.com, or contact sales@businessexpertpress.com.

www.ingramcontent.com/pod-product-compliance
Lightning Source LLC
Chambersburg PA
CBHW061150220326
41599CB00025B/4427